Nadiya's Kitcl Recipes for the Family

Flavorful Fusion Kitchen

Contents

INTRODUCTION

Nadiya's Kitchen: 98 Recipes for the Family is a cookbook like no other. This beautifully illustrated cookbook is authored by Nadiya Hussain, a Great British Bake-Off champion and author of top-selling cookbooks like Nadiya's British Food Adventure, Nadiya Bakes and Nadiya's Time to Eat. In Nadiya's Kitchen, Hussain has created a collection of recipes that you can prepare and serve to your entire family or even guests. Each of the 98 recipes is simple yet flavorsome, some of them taking cues from Hussain's unique Indian-Bangladeshi and British heritage. A few highlights from the book include the classic roast chicken, prawn biryani, banoffee ice cream cake, and coconut, cherry and cardamom chia seed pudding.

Nadiya's Kitchen is designed as a comprehensive guide to every family meal, from breakfasts to desserts. Overflowing with delicious, wholesome ingredients like brown rice, vegetables, chicken, seafood, and eggs, each recipe features easy-to-follow instructions. Health-conscious home cooks will appreciate that many of the recipes have been given a nutritional breakdown, including information on dietary requirements and key calorie information. Bright and vivid photographs depict the intricate yet achievable meal throughout the book.

The cookbook also features advice from Hussain on issues such as meal planning and time management, pantry staples and kitchen equipment. Whether you're a beginner or an experienced cook, Nadiya's Kitchen provides plenty of inspiration for the home chef in the family. With its combination of flavors, spices, and tried-and-tested recipes, this cookbook has something for everyone. With Hussain's encouraging words, and thoughtfully curated recipes, you'll enjoy turning your kitchen into a family-friendly space that everyone loves. So grab your copy of Nadiya's Kitchen: 98 Recipes for the Family, and get ready to start cooking.

1. Chicken Biryani

Chicken Biryani is a flavorful and delicious Indian dish, combining cooked chicken and fragrant basmati rice. It is a fairly easy-to-make meal that can be served for lunch or dinner.

Serving - 8-10 servings
Preparation Time - 20 minutes
Ready Time - 1 hour

Ingredients:
2 tablespoons vegetable oil
2 large onions, finely chopped
6 cloves garlic, finely minced
2 tablespoons grated ginger
2 teaspoons ground coriander
1 teaspoon ground turmeric
1 teaspoon ground cumin
1 teaspoon garam masala
2 green chilies, seeded and chopped
1 cup plain yogurt
4 large skinless chicken breasts, cut into cubes
2 cups basmati rice, rinsed and drained
3 cups chicken stock
1 teaspoon salt
2 tablespoons chopped coriander

Instructions:
1. Heat the oil in a large saucepan over medium heat. Add in the onions and cook until golden brown, then add in the garlic and ginger and stir to combine.
2. Add in the ground coriander, turmeric, cumin, and garam masala and continue stirring.
3. Add the green chilies and yogurt, and stir until everything is combined.
4. Add the chicken and cook until the chicken is no longer pink, about 10 minutes.
5. Add the rice and stir until it is combined with the other Ingredients.
6. Add the chicken stock and salt and bring the mixture to a boil.

7. Reduce the heat to low and cover the saucepan with a lid. Simmer for 25 minutes.

8. Remove from heat and let the biryani sit for about 10 minutes.

9. Sprinkle the chopped cilantro over the biryani before serving.

Nutrition information -
Calories: 308 calories; Total Fat: 11g; Cholesterol: 54mg; Sodium: 593mg; Total Carbohydrates: 29g; Protein: 20g

2. Chocolate Orange Cake

Chocolate Orange Cake is an indulgent, decadent way to finish off any meal. This particular recipe combines the flavors of chocolate and orange which bring out flavors that are amazing and surprisingly complementary.

Serving: 12
Preparation time: 20 minutes
Ready time: 40 minutes

Ingredients:
-2 sticks butter, softened
-1 cup granulated sugar
-3 eggs
-2 teaspoons orange extract
-2 cups all-purpose flour
-1 teaspoon baking powder
-3/4 cup cocoa powder
-2 teaspoons baking soda
-1/2 teaspoon salt
-1 cup buttermilk
-Orange zest

Instructions:
1. Preheat oven to 350 degrees and butter a 9-inch round cake pan.
2. In a large bowl, cream together butter and sugar until light and fluffy.
3. Beat in eggs, one at a time, and add orange extract.
4. In a separate bowl, whisk together flour, baking powder, cocoa powder, baking soda and salt.

5. Gradually add the dry Ingredients to the butter mixture, alternating with buttermilk, and stirring until completely combined.
6. Fold in orange zest and spread batter into prepared cake pan.
7. Bake for 30-40 minutes or until a toothpick inserted in the center comes out clean.
8. Allow cake to cool before frosting and serving.

Nutrition information (per serving): Calories: 325; Total Fat: 15 g; Saturated Fat: 9 g; Sodium: 259 mg; Carbohydrates: 44 g; Fiber: 2 g; Protein: 5 g

3. Lamb Curry

Lamb Curry is a spicy, fragrant stew originating from India. It is usually served over steamed rice or with fresh naan bread.
Serving: Serves 6
Preparation Time: 10 minutes
Ready Time: 45 minutes

Ingredients:
- 2 tbsp olive oil
- 4 cloves of garlic, minced
- 1 onion, diced
- 1 lb. boneless lamb, cut into cubes
- 1 tbsp garam masala
- 1 tsp turmeric
- 1/2 tsp cayenne pepper
- 28oz. can of diced tomatoes
- 1/2 cup Greek yogurt

Instructions:
1. Heat the olive oil over medium-high heat in a large pot.
2. Add the garlic and onion and sauté until softened, about 5 minutes.
3. Add the lamb cubes and season with garam masala, turmeric, and cayenne pepper. Cook for 8-10 minutes, stirring occasionally.
4. Pour in the diced tomatoes and bring to a simmer. Reduce heat to low and cover. Let simmer for 30 minutes.
5. Stir in the Greek yogurt and let simmer for an additional 5 minutes.

6. Serve over steamed rice or with fresh naan bread.

Nutrition information: Per Serving 168 calories, 11.2g fat, 5.7g carbohydrates, 6.3g protein.

4. Coconut Rice Pudding

Coconut Rice Pudding is a classic dessert that combines fragrant coconut milk with sweet, cooked rice for a delicious, creamy treat.
Serving: 6
Preparation time: 10 minutes
Ready time: 2 hours

Ingredients:
- 4 cups cooked jasmine or basmati rice
- 2 cups coconut milk
- 1/2 cup raisins
- 1/2 cup sugar
- 2 tablespoons butter
- 1 teaspoon salt
- 2 teaspoons vanilla extract

Instructions:
1. In a large saucepan over medium heat, melt the butter.
2. Add the cooked rice, coconut milk, raisins, sugar, salt, and vanilla extract. Stir to combine all Ingredients.
3. Reduce heat to low, cover, and cook for 1.5 hours, stirring occasionally.
4. Remove from heat and let cool before serving.

Nutrition information:
Calories: 297 kcal, Carbohydrates: 54 g, Protein: 4 g, Fat: 8 g, Saturated Fat: 6 g, Sodium: 356 mg, Potassium: 218 mg, Fiber: 2 g, Sugar: 23 g, Vitamin A: 81 IU, Vitamin C: 1 mg, Calcium: 29 mg, Iron: 2 mg

5. Beef Kebabs

These delicious beef kebabs will have everyone's mouths watering! Whether you choose to serve them as an appetizer or main course, these flavorful kebabs will be a hit with all your guests.

Serving: Serves 8
Preparation Time: 15 minutes
Ready Time: 30 minutes

Ingredients:
- 2 pounds ground beef
- 2 teaspoons ground cinnamon
- 2 tablespoons garlic powder
- 2 tablespoons paprika
- 2 tablespoons dried oregano
- 2 tablespoons ground cumin
- 1/2 teaspoon freshly ground black pepper
- 1/2 teaspoon salt
- 1 onion, finely chopped

Instructions:
1. In a large bowl, combine the ground beef, cinnamon, garlic powder, paprika, oregano, cumin, pepper and salt. Mix until all of the spices are evenly distributed in the beef.
2. Take about 2 tablespoons of the mixture and shape into a round shaped kebab. Do this for the rest of the beef mixture until all of the beef has been made into kebabs.
3. Heat a large skillet or grill pan over medium-high heat. Place the kebabs in the pan and cook for 4-5 minutes. Flip the kebabs and cook for an additional 4-5 minutes.
4. Serve the beef kebabs with the chopped onion.

Nutrition information: Calories: 400; Fat: 26g; Saturated Fat: 12g; Cholesterol: 88mg; Sodium: 291mg; Carbohydrates: 8g; Fiber: 2g; Sugar: 2g; Protein: 28g

6. Lemon Drizzle Traybake

Lemon Drizzle Traybake is a delicious and tangy lemon-flavored dessert that is sure to make your taste buds tingle. The light and airy texture of this treat makes it perfect for kids and adults alike.

Serving: 8

Preparation time: 15 minutes

Ready time: 1 hour

Ingredients:
- 2 cups plain flour
- 1 teaspoon baking powder
- ¾ cup caster sugar
- 1 teaspoon lemon zest
- 2 eggs
- ½ cup melted butter
- ½ cup milk
- ½ cup freshly squeezed lemon juice
- 1 tablespoon powdered sugar for decoration

Instructions:
1. Preheat oven to 350°F (175°C). Grease and flour an 8-inch square baking pan.
2. In a large bowl, combine flour, baking powder, caster sugar, and lemon zest.
3. In a separate bowl, whisk together eggs, melted butter, milk, and lemon juice.
4. Pour the wet Ingredients into the dry Ingredients and mix until everything is combined.
5. Pour the batter into the prepared baking pan and bake for 45 minutes.
6. When done, the cake should be golden brown. Let the cake cool before slicing.
7. Sprinkle with powdered sugar before serving.

Nutrition information: Each serving has approximately 210 calories, 8g of fat, 32g of carbohydrates, and 3g of protein.

7. Vegetable Biryani

Vegetable Biryani is a delicious and flavorful rice dish that is made with a mix of vegetables, spices, and herbs. It is a popular dish in the Indian subcontinent and is usually served as a main course for lunch or dinner.

Serving: 4-6

Preparation Time: 15 minutes

Ready Time: 45 minutes

Ingredients:

- 2 cups Basmati Rice
- 2 tablespoons oil
- 1 onion, sliced
- 500 gm of mix vegetables (peas, carrots, cauliflower, beans)
- 5-6 cloves of garlic, minced
- 1 tablespoon ginger, finely chopped
- 2 teaspoons cumin seeds
- 2 tablespoons coriander powder
- 1 teaspoon garam masala
- 1 teaspoon turmeric powder
- 2 tablespoons tomato puree
- 2 tablespoons all-purpose flour
- Salt to taste
- 2 tablespoons chopped mint and coriander leaves
- 1 green chili, chopped
-4-5 cups of water

Instructions:

1. Soak the Basmati rice for 10 minutes.
2. Heat two tablespoons of oil in a pan over medium heat and fry the onion until they are golden.
3. Add all the vegetables, garlic, ginger, cumin seeds, coriander powder, garam masala, turmeric powder, tomato puree, all-purpose flour, and salt to taste to the pan and stir-fry for 5 minutes.
4. Drain the Basmati rice and add it to the vegetables.
5. Pour 4-5 cups of water into the pan and bring the mixture to a boil.
6. Reduce the heat and cover the pan. Allow the rice and vegetables to cook for about 25 minutes, or until the rice is cooked and all the liquid has been absorbed.
7. Stir in the chopped mint and coriander leaves and the green chili before turning off the heat.

8. Serve the Vegetable Biryani hot with a side of your favorite accompaniment.

Nutrition information: (per serving)
Calories: 220 kcal
Carbohydrates: 36 g
Protein: 6 g
Fat: 7 g
Saturated Fat: 1 g
Cholesterol: 0 mg
Sodium: 50 mg
Potassium: 240 mg
Fiber: 4 g
Sugar: 5 g
Vitamin A: 25.9 %
Vitamin C: 21.2 %
Calcium: 7.4 %
Iron: 10.2 %

8. Spiced Apple Crumble

Spiced Apple Crumble is a delicious Fall dessert that combines spiced apples with a crispy cinnamon oat topping.
Serving: 8
Preparation Time: 15 minutes
Ready Time: 40 minutes

Ingredients:
Filling:
- 4 large apples (chopped into small pieces)
- 1/4 cup sugar
- 1 tsp ground cinnamon
- 1/4 cup water
Topping:
- 1 1/2 cups old-fashioned rolled oats
- 1/4 cup all-purpose flour
- 1/4 cup brown sugar
- 1 tsp ground cinnamon

- 1/4 cup unsalted butter (cold, cut into small pieces)

Instructions:
1. Preheat your oven to 350 degrees.
2. In a medium saucepan, combine the apples, sugar, cinnamon, and water. Stir until everything is combined.
3. Bring the mixture to a simmer over medium-high heat. Cook, stirring, until the apples are tender, about 10 minutes.
4. Meanwhile, make the topping. In a medium bowl, combine the oats, flour, sugar, and cinnamon. Add the butter and mix with your fingers until the mixture resembles fine crumbs.
5. Grease an 8-inch square baking dish. Pour the apple mixture into the baking dish. Spread the topping over the apples.
6. Bake for 20-25 minutes, or until the topping is golden and crispy.
7. Let cool before serving.

Nutrition information: Per Serving: Calories: 224, Total Fat: 8.7g, Saturated Fat: 5.1g, Cholesterol: 20mg, Sodium: 11mg, Total Carbohydrates: 34.6g, Dietary Fiber: 3.5g, Sugars: 18.9g, Protein: 2.9g

9. Butter Chicken

Butter Chicken is an Indian-style dish that features a creamy sauce made with butter and spices. Served over chicken and rice, it's a creamy comfort food that everyone can enjoy.
Serving: Serves 4
Preparation Time: 10 minutes
Ready Time: 40 minutes

Ingredients:
- 4 chicken breasts
- 2 cloves garlic, minced
- 1 tablespoon ginger, minced
- 2 tablespoons butter
- 2 tablespoons olive oil
- 2 cups tomato puree
- 1 cup whipping cream

- 1/2 teaspoon garam masala
- 1 teaspoon chili powder
- 1 teaspoon cumin
- 1 teaspoon Turmeric
- Salt to taste

Instructions:
1. Cut chicken into cubes and season with salt.
2. Heat butter and oil in a pan over medium heat.
3. Add minced garlic and ginger to pan and cook for a few minutes, stirring often.
4. Add chicken cubes to pan and cook until lightly browned.
5. Add tomato puree, whipping cream, garam masala, chili powder, cumin, and turmeric.
6. Simmer for a few minutes, stirring occasionally.
7. Reduce heat to low, cover, and simmer for 30 minutes.
8. Serve over cooked basmati rice.

Nutrition information: Calories: 308, Carbohydrates: 10 g, Protein: 27 g, Fat: 17 g, Cholesterol: 95 mg, Sodium: 228 mg, Potassium: 542 mg, Fiber: 1 g, Sugar: 5 g, Vitamin A: 722 IU, Vitamin C: 5 mg, Calcium: 52 mg, Iron: 2 mg

10. Banana Bread

Banana bread is an irresistible classic that can be enjoyed as a snack or dessert. It is made with ripe mashed bananas, flour, eggs, butter, and spices and then baked in a loaf pan.
Serving: 8
Preparation Time: 15 minutes
Ready Time: 1 hour

Ingredients:
- 3 ripe large bananas
- 1/3 cup melted butter
- 3/4 cup white sugar
- 1 teaspoon vanilla extract
- 1 teaspoon baking soda

- 2 cups all-purpose flour
- 1/2 teaspoon salt
- 1 teaspoon ground cinnamon
- 2 large eggs, lightly beaten

Instructions:
1. Preheat the oven to 350 degrees F (175 degrees C). Grease a 9x5 inch loaf pan.
2. In a large bowl, mash the bananas. Stir in the melted butter.
3. Add the sugar, vanilla, baking soda, flour, salt, and cinnamon. Mix in eggs until just blended.
4. Pour the batter into the prepared pan. Bake for 50 minutes to 1 hour at 350 degrees F (175 degrees C), or until a toothpick inserted into the center of the loaf comes out clean. Cool for 10 minutes before removing from the pan.

Nutrition information: Per Serving: 260 calories; 16.4 g fat; 28.3 g carbohydrates; 4.3 g protein; 63 mg cholesterol; 213 mg sodium.

11. Tandoori Chicken

Tandoori Chicken is an Indian dish made with a marinade of yogurt, ginger, garlic, spices, and lemon juice before it is roasted in a clay oven.
Serving: 4
Preparation time: 10 minutes
Ready time: 1 hour

Ingredients:
- 2 pounds of boneless, skinless chicken, cut into 1-inch pieces
- 1 cup plain yogurt
- 2 tablespoons ginger paste
- 2 tablespoons garlic paste
- 1 teaspoon garam masala spice blend
- 1 teaspoon ground cumin
- ½ teaspoon ground coriander
- Juice of 1 lemon
- 2 tablespoons vegetable oil

Instructions:
1. In a large bowl, combine the yogurt, ginger paste, garlic paste, garam masala, cumin, coriander, and lemon juice. Whisk together until evenly combined.
2. Add in the chicken pieces and stir to ensure they are well-coated in the marinade. Cover the bowl and let marinate in the refrigerator for at least 1 hour.
3. Preheat the oven to 400°F. Line a baking sheet with parchment paper and set aside.
4. Place the marinated chicken pieces onto the prepared baking sheet. Drizzle with the vegetable oil.
5. Bake for 25-30 minutes, or until the chicken is cooked through and golden brown.
6. Serve with rice or naan and enjoy!

Nutrition information: Per Serving: 225 calories; 10 g fat; 10 g carbohydrates; 24 g protein; 350 mg sodium.

12. Sticky Toffee Pudding

Sticky Toffee Pudding is a classic British dessert that is made with dates, covered in a toffee sauce and topped with a light, fluffy cake. It's the perfect sweet treat for after dinner.
Serving: Serves 6
Preparation Time: 15 minutes
Ready Time: 1 hour

Ingredients:
- 1 1/2 cups dates, pitted and roughly chopped
- 1 cup boiling water
- 4 tablespoons butter
- 1/2 cup dark brown sugar
- 1 1/2 cups all-purpose flour
- 1 teaspoon baking soda
- 2 eggs
- 2 teaspoons vanilla extract
- 2 tablespoons demerara (raw) sugar

Instructions:

1. Preheat your oven to 350°F.

2. Grease an 8-inch square baking dish.

3. In a medium bowl, combine the dates and boiling water. Set aside to cool slightly.

4. In a small pot, melt the butter and dark brown sugar together over medium heat. Simmer for 3 minutes.

5. In a large bowl, sift together the flour and baking soda.

6. To the flour mixture, add the eggs and vanilla extract and beat together.

7. Add the butter and sugar mixture and stir until smooth.

8. Stir in the date mixture.

9. Pour the batter into the prepared baking dish.

10. Sprinkle the demerara sugar over the top.

11. Bake for 35 minutes, or until a toothpick inserted in the center comes out clean.

12. Let cool on a wire rack for 10 minutes before serving.

Nutrition information: per serving: 260 kcal, 11.2 g fat, 35.9 g carbohydrates, 2.8 g protein

13. Aloo Gobi

Aloo Gobi is a popular Indian dish combining potatoes and cauliflower. This vegetarian side dish is flavorful and satisfying.
Serving: 6
Preparation Time: 10 minutes
Ready Time: 30 minutes

Ingredients:
- 2 tablespoons vegetable oil
- 1 teaspoon cumin seeds
- 2 garlic cloves, minced
- 1 teaspoon freshly grated ginger
- 1 teaspoon ground coriander
- ¼ teaspoon cayenne pepper
- 2 potatoes, cut into small cubes
- 1 large head of cauliflower, cut into florets

- 1 teaspoon garam masala
- ½ teaspoon turmeric
- 1 teaspoon salt
- 2 tablespoons chopped fresh cilantro

Instructions:
1. Heat the vegetable oil in a large, deep skillet over medium-high heat. Add the cumin seeds and cook until fragrant, about 30 seconds. Add the garlic, ginger, coriander, and cayenne pepper and cook for 1 minute.
2. Add the potatoes and cauliflower and cook, stirring frequently, for 5 minutes. Add the garam masala, turmeric, and salt and cook, stirring, for another 5 minutes or until the vegetables are tender.
3. Sprinkle with the cilantro and serve.

Nutrition information: Per serving: 188 calories, 10.6 g fat, 0.8 g saturated fat, 22.7 g carbohydrate, 3.3 g protein, 4.5 g fiber

14. Chocolate Brownies

Delicious, decadent chocolate brownies are an absolute must! These homemade brownies have a fantastic crackly top and a gooey center that will delight your family and friends.
Serving: 10-12 square brownies
Preparation time: 20 minutes
Ready time: 45 minutes

Ingredients:
- 2/3 cup all-purpose flour
- 2/3 cup cocoa powder
- 1/4 teaspoon baking powder
- 1/4 teaspoon salt
- 8 tablespoons unsalted butter
- 1/2 cup granulated sugar
- 1/3 cup light brown sugar
- 2 large eggs
- 1 teaspoon vanilla extract
- 1/2 cup semi-sweet chocolate chips

Instructions:

1. Preheat oven to 350°F. Grease an 8x8-inch square baking pan with nonstick cooking spray.
2. In a medium bowl, whisk together the flour, cocoa powder, baking powder, and salt.
3. In a separate large bowl, cream together butter, granulated sugar, and brown sugar until light and fluffy. Add eggs individually, beating between each and then mix until fully combined. Stir in the vanilla.
4. Add the flour mixture to the wet Ingredients and mix until just combined. Fold in the chocolate chips.
5. Pour the brownie batter into the prepared baking pan and spread evenly.
6. Bake for 30 minutes, or until a toothpick inserted in the middle comes out clean.
7. Let the brownies cool completely before slicing.

Nutrition information: per brownie (approx 1/12 of the recipe) - 154 calories, 7 g fat, 21 g carbohydrates, 2 g protein

15. Chicken Tikka Masala

Chicken Tikka Masala is highly flavorful Indian dish featuring marinated chicken cooked in a tomato-based sauce. It is one of the most popular dishes in Indian restaurants.

Serving: 4-5
Preparation Time: 30 minutes
Ready Time: 45 minutes

Ingredients:
• 2 lbs boneless skinless chicken breasts (cut into cubes)
• 1/2 red onion (finely chopped)
• 2 cloves garlic (minced)
• 2 tablespoons olive oil
• 2 tablespoons garam masala
• 2 tablespoons paprika
• 1 tablespoon freshly grated ginger
• 1 8oz can tomato sauce
• 2 tablespoons plain Greek yogurt

• Salt and pepper to taste

Instructions:
• In a bowl, combine the cubed chicken, red onion, garlic, olive oil, garam masala, paprika, ginger, and salt and pepper. Stir until the chicken is evenly coated.
• Heat a large skillet over medium heat. Add the chicken mixture and cook for about 8 minutes, stirring often, until the chicken is cooked through.
• Add the tomato sauce and cook for an additional 5 minutes.
• Reduce the heat to low and stir in the yogurt. Simmer for 2-3 minutes.
• Serve over warm basmati rice.

Nutrition information: Calories: 303; Protein: 38 g; Fat: 10 g; Carbohydrates: 15 g; Fiber: 3 g; Sodium: 297 mg

16. Carrot Cake

Carrot Cake is a classic, moist and fluffy cake filled with delicious spices and filled with carrots for a sweet surprise. This recipe is a guaranteed crowd-pleaser and is sure to become one of your favorite go-to recipes.
Serving: 10 - 12
Preparation time: 15 minutes
Ready time: 1 hour 10 minutes

Ingredients:
- 2 cups all-purpose flour
- 2 ½ teaspoons baking powder
- 2 teaspoons ground cinnamon
- ¼ teaspoon freshly grated nutmeg
- ¼ teaspoon baking soda
- ¼ teaspoon salt
- 2 cups light brown sugar, lightly packed
- ¾ cup vegetable oil
- 4 large eggs
- 2 cups grated carrots
- 1 cup chopped walnuts (optional)

Instructions:
1. Preheat oven to 350°F (177°C). Grease and lightly flour a 9x13 inch cake pan.
2. In a large bowl, whisk together the flour, baking powder, cinnamon, nutmeg, baking soda, and salt.
3. In another bowl, whisk together the brown sugar, oil, and eggs until light and creamy.
4. Gradually add the dry Ingredients to the wet Ingredients and mix until combined.
5. Fold in the grated carrots and chopped walnuts (optional).
6. Pour the batter into the prepared cake pan and spread evenly.
7. Bake in preheated oven for 45 minutes or until a toothpick inserted in the center comes out clean.
8. Allow to cool completely before serving.

Nutrition information: Per Serving: 182 kcal, 12.7g fat, 18.9g carbohydrates, 4.5g protein

17. Butter Paneer

Butter Paneer is a creamy, delicious curry made with cubes of cheese and Indian spices. It has a comforting flavor and is sure to please a variety of palates.
Serving: 6
Preparation Time: 15 minutes
Ready Time: 35 minutes

Ingredients:
-2 tablespoons butter
-1 onion, diced
-2 cloves garlic, minced
-2 teaspoons dried cumin
-1 teaspoon garam masala
-1 teaspoon turmeric
-1 teaspoon ground ginger
-1 (14 ounce) can tomato sauce
-1 cup heavy cream
-Salt and pepper, to taste

-1/2 teaspoon cayenne pepper
-1 pound paneer cheese, cubed
-2 tablespoons fresh cilantro, chopped

Instructions:
1. Heat the butter in a large saucepan over medium heat.
2. Add the onion and garlic and cook until softened, about 5 minutes.
3. Stir in the cumin, garam masala, turmeric, and ginger and cook for 1 minute.
4. Pour in the tomato sauce and stir to combine. Simmer for 10 minutes.
5. Add the cream to the sauce and stir to combine. Simmer for 5 minutes.
6. Season with salt, pepper, and cayenne pepper. Stir in the paneer and simmer for 10 minutes.
7. Garnish with cilantro and serve.

Nutrition information: Servings 6; Calories 382; Fat 25g; Saturated Fat 12g; Cholesterol 62mg; Sodium 242mg; Carbohydrates 16g; Fiber 1g; Protein 16g

18. Mango Lassi

Mango Lassi is a refreshing and creamy Indian yogurt-based smoothie. Enjoyed all over the world this is an easy and delicious summer cooler drink.
Serving: 4
Preparation time: 10 minutes
Ready time: 10 minutes

Ingredients:
- 1 cup plain yogurt
- 2-3 ripe mangoes (peeled and diced)
- 3 tablespoons honey
- 1/2 teaspoon cardamom powder
- 1/2 cup cold water
- 1/4 cup sliced almonds (optional)

Instructions:

1. In a blender, blend the yogurt, mangoes, honey, cardamom powder, and cold water until smooth.
2. Pour into glasses and top with almonds, if desired.
3. Serve and enjoy!

Nutrition information: Calories: 200; Fat: 3.5 g; Protein: 9 g; Carbohydrates: 36 g; Fiber: 3 g; Calcium: 200 mg; Sodium: 50 mg.

19. Lamb Biryani

Lamb Biryani is a spicy, flavorful and aromatic mix of rice, tender pieces of meat, and spices. It is one of the most popular recipes out of India, enjoyed by many around the world.
Serving: 8
Preparation Time: 25 minutes
Ready Time: 90 minutes

Ingredients:
- 2 lbs lamb, cut into small cubes
- 2 onions, diced
- 5 cloves garlic, minced
- 1 inch ginger, grated
- 2 tbsp olive oil
- 2 cups Basmati rice
- 6 cardamom pods
- 5 cloves
- 1 bay leaf
- 2 tsp turmeric
- 2 tsp garam masala
- 2 tsp coriander
- 2 cinnamon sticks
- 1 cup yogurt
- ½ cup milk
- ½ cup coriander leaves, chopped
- 1 cup shelled frozen peas
- ½ tsp chili powder
- Salt to taste

Instructions:
1. Heat olive oil in a large pot and sauté the garlic, ginger, and onions until lightly browned.
2. Add in the lamb cubes and cook until lightly browned.
3. Add in the spices and mix together.
4. Pour in the yogurt and milk and stir to combine. Add in the coriander leaves.
5. Add in the peas and chili powder.
6. Add in the Basmati rice and stir to combine.
7. Add the desired amount of salt.
8. Cover the pot and cook on medium-low heat for 40 minutes.
9. Remove from heat and serve.

Nutrition information: Calories: 462, Fat: 19g, Protein: 24g, Carbohydrates: 47g, Fiber: 4g, Sugars: 5g, Sodium: 9mg, Cholesterol: 77mg.

20. Victoria Sponge Cake

A Victoria Sponge Cake is an English cake traditionally filled with raspberry jam and whipped cream. It's named after Queen Victoria and is simple to make.
Serving: Makes one 8-inch-diameter cake (8-10 servings)
Preparation Time: 15 minutes
Ready Time: 35 minutes

Ingredients:
• 2/3 cup butter, at room temperature
• 2/3 cup white sugar
• 3 large eggs
• 2 tsp vanilla extract
• 2 cups all-purpose flour
• 1 1/2 tsp baking powder
• 1/4 tsp baking soda
• 1/2 tsp salt
• 2/3 cup buttermilk, or as needed
• 2/3 cup raspberry jam
• 1 cup heavy cream

Instructions:
1. Preheat oven to 350°F. Grease and line the bottom of an 8-inch round cake pan.
2. In a large bowl, cream together butter and sugar until light and fluffy. Add eggs one at a time, beating well after each addition. Add vanilla extract and stir to combine.
3. In a separate bowl, mix together the flour, baking powder, baking soda, and salt. Add the flour mixture to the butter mixture, alternating with the buttermilk, until the batter is smooth and creamy.
4. Pour the batter into the prepared pan and bake for 25-30 minutes, or until the cake is lightly golden and a toothpick inserted into the center comes out clean.
5. Let the cake cool in the pan for 10 minutes, then remove to a cooling rack to cool completely.
6. Once cooled, spread the raspberry jam over one layer and whip the cream until light and fluffy. Spread the cream over the jam layer and top with the remaining cake layer.

Nutrition information:Per Serving (1/10 of cake): 367 calories, 12.8 g fat, 4.8 g saturated fat, 57.6 g carbohydrates, 2.5 g protein, 4.3 g fiber, 170 mg sodium

21. Chicken Korma

Chicken Korma is an Indian dish with tender pieces of chicken cooked in a creamy and spicy sauce, combined with flavorful spices, coconut, and curry. The dish is traditionally served with pulao or naan bread for a delicious and comforting dinner.
Serving: 4
Preparation Time: 20 minutes
Ready Time: 50 minutes

Ingredients:
-1 teaspoon ground cardamom
-1 teaspoon ground cinnamon
-1/4 teaspoon ground cloves
-1/4 teaspoon ground nutmeg

-1 tablespoon ginger paste
-1 tablespoon garlic paste
-1 teaspoon turmeric
-1 teaspoon garam masala
-1½ teaspoons salt
-2 tablespoons vegetable oil
-2 small onions (finely chopped)
-2 tablespoons tomato paste
-1 cup plain yogurt
-1 fresh green chili pepper (finely chopped)
-1 lb chicken breast (cut into cubes)
-1/2 cup coconut cream
-1/2 cup water

Instructions:
1. In a small bowl, mix together the cardamom, cinnamon, cloves, nutmeg, ginger paste, garlic paste, turmeric, garam masala, and salt.
2. Heat the oil in a large saucepan over low heat. Add the onions and cook, stirring continually, until softened (4-5 minutes).
3. Add the spice mixture and tomato paste and stir to combine. Cook for 1 minute.
4. Pour in the yogurt and increase the heat to medium. Cook, stirring frequently, until lightly browned (4-5 minutes).
5. Add the chicken and chili pepper. Cook, stirring often, until the chicken is almost cooked through (8-10 minutes).
6. Add the coconut cream and water. Cook, stirring occasionally, until the chicken is cooked through and the sauce has thickened (10-15 minutes).
7. Serve the Chicken Korma with pulao or naan bread.

Nutrition information:
Calories: 340, Total Fat: 19g, Saturated Fat: 9g, Sodium: 620mg, Total Carbohydrate: 13g, Dietary Fiber: 3g, Protein: 29g

22. Raspberry Cheesecake

Delicious and creamy Raspberry Cheesecake is perfect for any special occasion or just for an anytime treat. Great for a birthday, anniversary or holiday, this dessert will be the hit of the party!

Serving: 8-10

Preparation time: 30 minutes

Ready time: 1-2 hours

Ingredients:
- 2 packages (8 ounces each) cream cheese, softened
- 3/4 cup sugar
- 1 teaspoon vanilla extract
- 3 eggs
- 1 graham cracker crust
- 1/2 cup raspberry preserves
- 1/4 teaspoon almond extract

Instructions:
- Preheat oven to 350°F.
- In a large bowl, beat cream cheese, sugar and vanilla until smooth.
- Add eggs, one at a time, beating on low speed just until blended.
- Place graham cracker crust in 9-inch springform pan.
- Pour cream cheese mixture into crust.
- Top with raspberry preserves.
- Bake for 45-55 minutes, or until center is almost set.
- Remove from oven and let cool to room temperature before refrigerating for 1-2 hours.

Nutrition information:
- Calories: 290
- Total Fat: 17g
- Sodium: 200mg
- Protein: 4g

23. Chana Masala

Chana Masala is a popular and flavorful North Indian dish that is made with chickpeas and simmered in a fragrant curry sauce.

Serving: 4

Preparation time: 45 minutes
Ready time:1 hour

Ingredients:
-2 tablespoons of vegetable oil
-2 bay leaves
-1 teaspoon cumin seeds
-1 teaspoon ground coriander
-1 teaspoon turmeric powder
-1 teaspoon garam masala
-2 cloves garlic, minced
-1 inch piece of ginger, minced
-2 green chilies, chopped
-1 large onion, chopped
-1 teaspoon of well-dried amchoor or 1 tablespoon of freshly squeezed lemon juice
-2 cans of chickpeas, drained and rinsed
-1/2 teaspoon of dry fenugreek leaves
-1 teaspoon of salt
-4 tomatoes, chopped
-1/2 cup of water
-1/4 cup of cilantro leaves, chopped

Instructions:
1. Heat the oil in a pan over medium-high heat.
2. Add the bay leaves and cumin seeds and fry for 1 minute.
3. Add the coriander, turmeric, garam masala, garlic, ginger, and green chilies to the pan and fry for another minute.
4. Add the onion and cook for 5 minutes, until softened.
5. Add the amchoor or lemon juice and fry for 15 seconds.
6. Add the chickpeas, fenugreek leaves, salt and tomatoes and stir to combine.
7. Add the water, cover and simmer for 25 minutes on low heat until the sauce is thickened.
8. Uncover, add the cilantro leaves and cook for further 5 minutes.
9. Serve warm with rice or naan.

Nutrition information: serving size of 1 cup (300 g):
Calories: 207
Fat: 7 g

Carbs: 27 g
Protein: 9 g

24. Baklava

Baklava is a delicious nut-filled pastry that has origins in the Middle Eastern and Mediterranean cuisines, but is now widely enjoyed across the world.
Serving: 24 pieces
Preparation Time: 15 minutes
Ready Time: 1 hour

Ingredients:
- 1/2 pound unsalted butter
- 1 pound phyllo dough
- 3 cups finely chopped walnuts
- 1/4 cup sugar
- 1 teaspoon ground cinnamon
- 2 teaspoons freshly grated lemon zest
- Honey, for garnish

Instructions:
1. Preheat the oven to 350 degrees Fahrenheit.
2. Melt the butter and set it aside.
3. Grease a 9x13 inch baking pan with some of the butter.
4. Layer 8 - 10 sheets of phyllo dough in the pan, brushing each sheet with butter.
5. In a separate bowl, mix the walnuts, sugar, cinnamon, and lemon zest.
6. Sprinkle about 2 tablespoons of the walnut mixture over the phyllo sheets.
7. Repeat layering the phyllo dough and walnut mixture until all the Ingredients are used.
8. Cut the pastries into 24 triangles, using a sharp knife.
9. Bake for 25 to 30 minutes, until golden brown.
10. Let cool, then drizzle with honey.

Nutrition information: Per Serving: 241 calories; 13.4 g fat; 28.4 g carbohydrates; 4.1 g protein; 11 mg cholesterol; 104 mg sodium.

25. Vegetable Curry

Vegetable Curry is a flavorful and hearty stew made with a mix of various vegetables, spices, and seasonings. This delicious and nutritious dish is a great way to get your daily dose of vegetables.

Serving: 4-6
Preparation Time: 15 minutes
Ready Time: 45 minutes

Ingredients:

- 1 tablespoon vegetable oil
- 1 small onion, chopped
- 3 cloves garlic, minced
- 1 tablespoon ginger, grated
- 2-3 tablespoons curry powder
- 2 large potatoes, cut into cubes
- 2 cups vegetables such as carrots, green beans, peppers, etc.
- 2 cups vegetable broth
- 1 can diced tomatoes
- 1 teaspoon salt
- 1/2 teaspoon pepper
- 2 tablespoons fresh cilantro, chopped

Instructions:

1. Heat oil in a large pot over medium heat.
2. Add the onion and garlic and cook for 2-3 minutes.
3. Add the ginger and curry powder and cook for 1 minute more.
4. Add the potatoes and vegetables and cook for 3-4 minutes.
5. Add the broth, tomatoes, salt, and pepper.
6. Bring the pot to a boil, then reduce heat and simmer for 30 minutes.
7. Stir in the cilantro and simmer for 5 more minutes.

Nutrition information: Serving size 1/4 of recipe. Calories: 130, Total fat: 4 g, Saturated fat: 0 g, Cholesterol: 0 mg, Sodium: 560 mg, Total carbohydrate: 24 g, Dietary fiber: 4 g, Protein: 3 g.

26. Chocolate Chip Cookies

Delicious, classic, and always a crowd pleaser, this Chocolate Chip Cookie recipe produces soft and chewy treats.
Serving: Makes 24 cookies
Preparation time: 15 minutes
Ready time: 30 minutes

Ingredients:
- 1 cup (2 sticks) unsalted butter, melted
- 1 cup packed light-brown sugar
- 1/2 cup granulated sugar
- 2 large eggs
- 2 teaspoons pure vanilla extract
- 2 1/4 cups all-purpose flour
- 1 teaspoon baking soda
- 1 teaspoon salt
- 2 cups semisweet chocolate chips

Instructions:
1. Preheat oven to 350 degrees. Line two baking sheets and set aside.
2. In a medium bowl, whisk melted butter and sugars until combined. Whisk in eggs and vanilla.
3. In a separate bowl, mix together flour, baking soda, and salt.
4. Slowly mix dry Ingredients into wet until combined. Stir in chocolate chips.
5. Using a medium ice-cream scoop, scoop rounded cookie dough onto the prepared baking sheets.
6. Bake for 10 to 12 minutes, or until edges are golden.
7. Cool on baking sheets 5 minutes before transferring to a wire rack to cool completely.

Nutrition information: Calories per serving: 170; Total Fat: 8.3g; Saturated Fat: 5.3g; Sodium: 107mg; Carbohydrates: 2.3g; Fiber: 0.6g; Protein: 1.2g

27. Chicken Curry

This rich and flavourful Chicken Curry is a go-to simple dinner recipe that takes only 30 minutes to prepare.
Serving: 4
Preparation Time: 10 minutes
Ready Time: 20 minutes

Ingredients:
- 3 tablespoons vegetable oil
- 1 kg chicken fillets, cut into bite-sized pieces
- ½ teaspoon turmeric
- 2 cloves garlic, minced
- 1 teaspoon ginger, minced
- 2 onions, diced
- 2 tablespoons tomato puree
- 2 ½ tablespoons curry powder
- 1 teaspoon paprika
- 250ml chicken stock
- 500g boiled potatoes

Instructions:
1. Heat oil in a large pan over medium heat. Add chicken and cook until lightly browned.
2. Add turmeric, garlic, ginger and onions to the pan and stir for 2-3 minutes.
3. Add tomato puree, curry powder and paprika and stir for 1-2 minutes.
4. Pour in the chicken stock and bring to a simmer.
5. Add the boiled potatoes and cook for 10 minutes.
6. Serve with rice or naan bread.

Nutrition information (per serving): protein 28, carbohydrates 19, fat 17, fibre 0.8, energy 250 kcal.

28. Apple Pie

Apple Pie is a delicious dessert perfect for any occasion. Its delightful combination of sweet and tart apples and hint of cinnamon make it a classic and timeless favorite.
Serving: 8

Preparation Time: 25 minutes
Ready Time: 65 minutes

Ingredients:
- 5 large Granny Smith apples, peeled and sliced
- 2/3 cup white sugar
- 2/3 cup packed light brown sugar
- 1/4 cup all-purpose flour
- 1 teaspoon ground cinnamon
- 1/4 teaspoon ground nutmeg
- 1/4 teaspoon salt
- 1 lemon, juiced
- 2 tablespoons unsalted butter
- 2 tablespoons water
- 9 inch unbaked pie crust

Instructions:
1. Preheat oven to 375°F (190°C).
2. In a large bowl, combine the sliced apples, white sugar, brown sugar, flour, cinnamon, nutmeg, salt, lemon juice, butter, and water; mix together until evenly blended.
3. Place apples in the unbaked 9 inch pie crust.
4. Bake in preheated oven for 40 to 50 minutes until golden brown.
5. Let cool for 15 minutes before serving.

Nutrition information: Per Serving - Calories: 411; Total Fat: 15g; Sodium: 190mg; Potassium: 103mg; Carbohydrates: 65g; Fiber: 4g; Sugar: 37g; Protein: 2g;

29. Prawn Biryani

Prawn Biryani is a popular Indian dish that combines succulent prawns with fragrant spices, herbs, and rice. This scrumptious meal is perfect for a weeknight dinner and is sure to impress your family and guests.
Serving: 4
Preparation time: 15 minutes
Ready time: 45 minutes

Ingredients:

-1 lb. large prawns, peeled and deveined
-2 cups Basmati rice, washed and soaked in water for 30 minutes
-2 tablespoons ghee
-2 onions, diced
-2 cups tomato puree
-1 tablespoon garlic paste
-1 teaspoon red chili powder
-1 teaspoon cumin powder
-1 teaspoon coriander powder
-1/2 teaspoon turmeric powder
-1 teaspoon garam masala
-1 teaspoon sea salt
-2 tablespoons chopped fresh cilantro
-2 tablespoons chopped fresh mint
-1/2 cup yogurt

Instructions:

1. Heat the ghee in a large pan over medium heat.
2. Add the onions and sauté until golden brown.
3. Add the garlic paste and sauté for another 2 minutes.
4. Add the tomato puree, red chili powder, cumin powder, coriander powder, turmeric powder, garam masala, and sea salt and mix well.
5. Cook the mixture until the oil begins to separate from the spices and tomatoes.
6. Add the prawns and cook until they are cooked through.
7. Drain the water from the soaked rice. Add the rice to the pan and stir to combine.
8. Add 2 cups of water to the pan and bring to a boil. Reduce the heat to medium-low, cover the pan and cook for 10 minutes.
9. Add the fresh cilantro, mint, and yogurt. Stir to combine. Cover the pan and cook for another 10 minutes until the rice is cooked through.
10. Serve the prawn biryani hot with a raita or your favorite condiments.

Nutrition information:

Calories: 432, Total Fat: 11g, Saturated Fat: 3g, Cholesterol: 216 mg, Sodium: 538 mg, Potassium: 595 mg, Total Carbohydrates: 58g, Dietary Fiber: 3g, Sugar: 9g, Protein: 21g

30. Black Forest Gateau

Black Forest Gateau is a chocolate-based cake that originated in Germany. It comes with layers of chocolate cake, cream and cherries wrapped in chocolate frosting.
Serving: 8
Preparation time: 25 minutes
Ready time: 1 hour 30 minutes

Ingredients:
- 3/4 cup all-purpose flour
- 1/8 teaspoon baking soda
- 1/4 teaspoon baking powder
- 1/2 teaspoon salt
- 6 ounces bittersweet chocolate, chopped
- 1/2 cup (1 stick) butter
- 4 eggs
- 1 cup granulated sugar
- 1 teaspoon vanilla extract
- 1 cup (8 ounces) sour cream
- 3/4 cup heavy cream
- 2 tablespoons kirschwasser (clear cherry brandy)
- 2 cups sweetened flaked coconut
- 1 (21-ounce) can cherry pie filling

Instructions:
1. Preheat oven to 350°F. Grease and flour two 8-inch cake pans.
2. In a medium bowl, whisk together flour, baking soda, baking powder and salt; set aside.
3. In the top of a double boiler, melt chocolate and butter.
4. In a large bowl, beat eggs and sugar with a hand mixer until thick and pale. Beat in melted chocolate and vanilla.
5. With a rubber spatula, gently fold in the dry Ingredients. Add sour cream and mix until just combined. Divide the batter between the prepared pans.
6. Bake for 25 minutes, or until a wooden pick inserted into the center of the cake comes out clean. Cool the cakes in the pans on a wire rack for 10 minutes. Carefully flip out the cakes onto the wire rack to cool completely.

7. Whip heavy cream to stiff peaks in the bowl of a standing mixer. Fold in kirschwasser. Place one cake layer on a serving plate. Spread with half of the whipped cream. Sprinkle with half of the coconut then top with half of the cherry pie filling. Place second cake layer on top. Spread with remaining whipped cream, coconut and cherry pie filling.

Nutrition information: Calories: 400, Fat: 20g, Carbohydrates: 49g, Protein: 6g, Sodium: 225mg, Cholesterol: 80mg, Fiber: 3g, Sugar: 34g

31. Beef Curry

Beef Curry is an exotic and flavorful Indian dish. This hearty, spicy curry packs a rich intense flavor and can be enjoyed along with steamed basmati rice, or naan.
Serving: 4-6
Preparation Time: 30 minutes
Ready Time: 1 hour

Ingredients:
-3 tablespoons of oil
-2 pounds of beef, cubed
-1 onion, diced
-2 garlic cloves, minced
-1 teaspoon ground ginger
-2 teaspoons ground cumin
-2 teaspoons ground coriander
-1 teaspoon ground cinnamon
-2 teaspoons of garam masala
-3 teaspoons of salt
-1 teaspoon of black pepper
-1 teaspoon of cayenne pepper
-1/4 cup tomato paste
-1 cup of water

Instructions:
1. Heat oil in a large skillet over medium-high heat.
2. Add beef cubes, onion, and garlic, and cook until beef is browned.

3. Add in all the spices and seasonings, including ginger, cumin, coriander, cinnamon, garam masala, salt, pepper, cayenne, and tomato paste.

4. Stir Ingredients together and cook for two minutes.

5. Pour in a cup of water and reduce heat to medium-low.

6. Cover the pan and cook for 45 minutes until meat is tender.

7. Uncover and simmer for an additional 15 minutes until sauce has thickened.

Nutrition information:
Calories: 330
Fat: 16 g
Carbohydrates: 11 g
Fiber: 3
Protein: 33 g
Sodium: 1400 mg

32. Lemon Meringue Pie

Lemon Meringue Pie is a classic and favorite dessert. This recipe is simple and straightforward – perfect for any occasion!
Serving: 10
Preparation time: 45 minutes
Ready time: 1 hour

Ingredients:
• 2 cups all-purpose flour
• 3/4 cup sugar
• 1/4 teaspoon salt
• 2 sticks cold butter, diced
• 1 large egg
• 2 tablespoons ice water
• 4 large egg yolks
• 3/4 cup freshly squeezed lemon juice
• 1 1/2 tablespoons grated lemon zest
• 1/3 cup heavy cream
• 4 large egg whites
• 1/4 teaspoon cream of tartar

• 1/3 cup sugar

Instructions:
1. Preheat oven to 350°F.
2. In a large bowl, whisk together 2 cups flour, 3/4 cup sugar, and 1/4 teaspoon salt. Add butter pieces and use a pastry blender to cut butter into dry Ingredients until it resembles coarse meal.
3. In a small bowl, lightly beat 1 egg with 2 tablespoons of ice water. Add egg mixture to flour and butter mixture and mix until mixture is combined. Wrap dough in plastic wrap and refrigerate for 30 minutes.
4. Roll out chilled dough on a lightly floured surface, about 1/8 inch thick, and press into a 9-inch pie dish. Trim off any excess dough. Pre-bake the crust for 15 minutes.
5. In a medium bowl, whisk together egg yolks, lemon juice, and lemon zest.
6. In a small saucepan, heat cream over medium heat and slowly pour it into the egg yolk and lemon juice mixture, whisking constantly.
7. Fill the pre-baked crust with lemon custard mixture and bake for 13 minutes.
8. In a large bowl, beat egg whites with a mixer until foamy. Add cream of tartar, then gradually add sugar while continuing to mix until glossy and soft peaks form.
9. Remove pie from oven and spread meringue over lemon custard. Return to oven and bake for an additional 18 minutes.
10. Cool pie to room temperature before serving.

Nutrition information:
Serving size: 1 slice of pie
Calories: 420 calories
Carbohydrates: 46 g
Sugar: 27 g
Fat: 22 g
Protein: 6 g
Cholesterol: 141 mg
Sodium: 146 mg
Fiber: 1 g

33. Saag Paneer

Saag Paneer is an Indian dish from the Punjab region. It is a combination of spinach (saag) and paneer (soft cottage cheese)in a thick curry sauce.
Serving: 4
Preparation Time: 10 minutes
Ready Time: 20 minutes

Ingredients:
- 250 g paneer (cubed)
- 2-3 cups of washed and chopped spinach
- 2 onions (chopped)
- 4 tablespoons vegetable oil
- 2 teaspoons ground cumin
- 1 teaspoon ground turmeric
- 2 teaspoons garam masala
- 1 teaspoon chili powder
- 4 cloves of garlic (minced)
- 2 tablespoons grated ginger
- 2 tablespoons chopped fresh cilantro
- 2 teaspoons sugar
- Salt to taste

Instructions:
1. Heat the oil in a large pan over medium-high heat.
2. Add the onions and fry until golden brown.
3. Add the cumin, turmeric, garam masala, and chili powder and fry for another few minutes.
4. Add the garlic and ginger and fry for another 2-3 minutes.
5. Add the chopped spinach and cook until wilted.
6. Add the cubes of paneer and cook for 5 minutes.
7. Add the sugar and salt, and stir to combine.
8. Cook for another few minutes until the sauce has thickened.
9. Serve with naan or basmati rice.

Nutrition information:
Calories: 256 kcal, Carbohydrates: 10 g, Protein: 11 g, Fat: 19 g, Saturated Fat: 7 g, Sodium: 856 mg, Potassium: 200 mg, Fiber: 2 g, Sugar: 4 g, Vitamin A: 5134 IU, Vitamin C: 24 mg, Calcium: 257 mg, Iron: 2 mg

34. Mango Sorbet

Enjoy the exciting flavor of Mango Sorbet with this easy and quick recipe.
Serving: Serves 8.
Preparation time: 10 minutes.
Ready time: 2 hours.

Ingredients:
- 2 mangoes, peeled and diced
- 1 cup of sugar
- 2 tablespoons of lime juice
- 2 cups of water

Instructions:
1. In a shallow dish combine the diced mangoes with the sugar and lime juice. Stir until the mixture is thick and sticky.
2. In a pan, combine the water with the mango mixture and bring to a light boil.
3. Simmer on low heat for 10 to 15 minutes, stirring occasionally.
4. Let cool completely in the pan before transferring to an airtight container or mold.
5. Store in the refrigerator for 1 to 2 hours or until completely chilled.
6. Scoop out of the mold with an ice cream scoop and serve.

Nutrition information:
Calories: 91 kcal
Carbohydrates: 22.2g
Protein: 0.9g
Fat: 0.2g
Cholesterol: 0 mg
Sodium: 0 mg
Fiber: 1.1g
Sugar: 19.3g

35. Chicken Shawarma

Chicken Shawarma is a classic Middle-Eastern dish featuring flavors of cardamom, sumac, and garlic. Thinly-sliced chicken is marinated in these spices before being grilled to perfection and wrapped in a warm pocket of pita bread.

Serving: 2-3

Preparation Time: 10 minutes

Ready Time: 40 minutes

Ingredients:
- 2 lb boneless, skinless chicken thighs, thinly sliced
- 2 cloves garlic, minced
- 2 teaspoons ground cardamom
- 1 teaspoon ground sumac
- 1 teaspoon ground cumin
- 1 teaspoon ground cinnamon
- 2 tablespoons olive oil
- 2 tablespoons fresh lemon juice
- Salt and freshly ground black pepper to taste
- 2-3 pita breads
- 2-3 tablespoons Greek yogurt
- Shredded lettuce
- Chopped tomatoes
- Sliced red onions

Instructions:
1. In a large bowl, combine the chicken thighs, garlic, cardamom, sumac, cumin, cinnamon, olive oil, lemon juice, salt, and pepper. Mix to combine.
2. Cover and refrigerate for at least 30 minutes, or up to 8 hours.
3. Preheat the grill to medium-high heat.
4. Grill the chicken thighs for 5-7 minutes, until cooked through and slightly charred.
5. To assemble the shawarma, warm the pita breads in the grill for 1-2 minutes.
6. Place the chicken in the center of the pita breads, top with Greek yogurt, lettuce, tomatoes, and onions.
7. Fold the ends of the pita breads up and enjoy.

Nutrition information:

Calories: 347, Total Fat: 17g, Saturated Fat: 4g, Cholesterol: 109mg, Sodium: 310mg, Carbohydrates: 24g, Fiber: 4g, Sugar: 3g, Protein: 28g

36. Red Velvet Cake

A delicious Red Velvet Cake with cream cheese frosting is a perfectly moist and tender cake that is sure to satisfy any sweet tooth.
Serving: 8-10
Preparation Time: 15 minutes
Ready Time: 1 hour

Ingredients:
- 2 ½ cups all-purpose flour
- 2 tablespoons cocoa powder
- 1 teaspoon baking powder
- ½ teaspoon baking soda
- ½ teaspoon salt
- ¾ cup (1 ½ sticks) unsalted butter
- 2 cups granulated sugar
- 3 large eggs
- ½ cup vegetable oil
- 1½ teaspoons pure vanilla extract
- 1 bottle (1 ounce) liquid red food coloring
- 1 cup buttermilk

Instructions:
1. Preheat oven to 350 degrees F (175 degrees C). Grease and flour two 9-inch round cake pans.
2. In a medium bowl, whisk together flour, cocoa powder, baking powder, baking soda and salt.
3. In a large bowl, cream together butter and sugar until light and fluffy. Beat in eggs one at a time until well incorporated.
4. Gradually add in the vegetable oil, vanilla extract and red food coloring, and mix until blended.
5. Alternate adding in the flour mixture and buttermilk and mix until combined.
6. Divide the cake batter between the prepared pans and spread evenly.

7. Bake in preheated oven for 30 minutes, or until a toothpick inserted into the center of the cakes comes out clean.

8. Allow cakes to cool for 10 minutes before turning out onto a wire rack to cool completely.

Nutrition information: Each slice of Red Velvet Cake contains approximately 540 calories, 26 grams of fat, 66 grams of carbohydrates, and 6 grams of protein.

37. Palak Paneer

Palak paneer is an Indian dish made with cooked spinach and cubes of cheese. It is a popular dish throughout the Indian subcontinent and has a flavorful, creamy texture.

Serving: 4-5

Preparation time: 15 minutes

Ready time: 40 minutes

Ingredients:
- 2 tablespoons of oil/ butter
- 1 teaspoon cumin seeds
- 1 teaspoon finely chopped garlic
- 1/2 teaspoon red chilli powder
- 1/2 teaspoon turmeric powder
- 2 cups chopped onion
- 2 cups chopped tomatoes
- 1 teaspoon garam masala
- 3 cups chopped spinach
- 1 block of paneer, cubed
- Salt to taste

Instructions:

1. Heat the oil or butter in a pan over medium heat and add the cumin seeds.

2. Once the cumin begins to sizzle, add the garlic and cook for 1-2 minutes.

3. Add the red chilli powder, turmeric powder, onion, and tomatoes and cook until the tomatoes are soft and the onions are lightly browned.

4. Add the garam masala and stir to combine.

5. Add the spinach and cook for 5 minutes, stirring occasionally.

6. Add the cubed paneer and season with salt. Cook for an additional 5 minutes.

7. Serve hot.

Nutrition information:
Calories: 233kcal
Fat: 17.1g
Carbohydrate: 11.3g
Protein: 10.1g
Fiber: 3.4g

38. Pistachio Ice Cream

Create a delectable frozen treat with this irresistible Pistachio Ice Cream recipe. This homemade ice cream is made with just four simple ingredients, and it's stuffed with lovely flavor thanks to the crushed pistachio nuts. Enjoy it as a sweet summer dessert.
Serving: Makes 8 servings.
Preparation Time: 25 minutes
Ready Time: 4 hours

Ingredients:
• 2 cups whole milk
• 2 cups heavy cream
• 1 cup granulated sugar
• 2 teaspoons vanilla
• 1/2 cup crushed pistachio nuts

Instructions:
1. In a blender, combine milk, cream, sugar, and vanilla. Blend on low speed until sugar is dissolved, about 1 minute.

2. Pour the mixture into an ice cream maker and follow the manufacturer's instructions to churn for 20 minutes.

3. After churning is complete, stir in the crushed pistachio nuts.

4. Cover and transfer the ice cream to a resealable container and freeze for at least 4 hours before serving.

Nutrition information

Serving Size: 1/2 cup
Calories: 279
Fat: 18g
Carbohydrates: 26g
Protein: 4g
Sodium: 28 mg

39. Lamb Kofta

Lamb Kofta is an Indo-Mediterranean dish made with seasoned ground meat that is typically shaped into cylinder or meatballs.
Serving: 4-6
Preparation Time: 15 minutes
Ready Time: 40 minutes

Ingredients:
- 500g ground lamb
- 3 cloves garlic, minced
- 1/2 teaspoon ground cumin
- 1/2 teaspoon ground coriander
- 1 teaspoon paprika
- 1/4 cup chopped flat-leaf parsley
- 1/4 cup chopped mint leaves
- 1/4 teaspoon ground black pepper
- 2 tablespoons olive oil
- 2 tablespoons plain yogurt
- Salt to taste

Instructions:
1. In a large bowl, combine the ground lamb, garlic, cumin, coriander, paprika, parsley, mint, pepper, olive oil, yogurt, and salt.
2. Mix the Ingredients together with your hands until they are fully incorporated.
3. Shape the mixture into cylinders or small meatballs.
4. Heat a large skillet over medium-high heat and add the koftas.
5. Cook for 10-15 minutes, turning regularly to ensure even cooking.

6. Serve with your favorite side dishes.

Nutrition information:
Calories: 210 kCal
Protein: 14.5 g
Carbohydrates: 4.0 g
Fat: 16 g

40. Blueberry Pancakes

Blueberry pancakes are fluffy, moist, and delicious pancakes topped with fresh or frozen blueberries. Enjoy this sweet breakfast treat with a generous pour of pure maple syrup!
Serving: Makes 12 Pancakes
Preparation Time: 10 minutes
Ready Time: 15 minutes

Ingredients:
• 2 cups all-purpose flour
• 2 teaspoons baking powder
• 1/4 teaspoon baking soda
• 1/4 teaspoon salt
• 2 eggs, lightly beaten
• 2 tablespoons honey
• 2 cups buttermilk
• 1/4 cup melted butter
• 2 teaspoons vanilla extract
• 1 cup blueberries (fresh or frozen)

Instructions:
1. In a large bowl, whisk together the flour, baking powder, baking soda, and salt.
2. In a separate bowl, whisk together the eggs, honey, buttermilk, melted butter, and vanilla extract until fully combined.
3. Pour the wet Ingredients into the bowl with the dry Ingredients and stir until just combined.
4. Gently fold the blueberries into the batter.

5. Heat a large skillet over medium heat and lightly grease with butter or cooking spray.

6. Pour 1/4 cup of pancake batter into the skillet. Cook until the edges begin to brown, about 3 minutes, then flip and cook for another 2-3 minutes.

7. Repeat with the remaining pancake batter. Serve with more blueberries and maple syrup.

Nutrition information:

Calories: 114 kcal, Carbohydrates: 16 g, Protein: 4 g, Fat: 4 g, Saturated Fat: 2 g, Cholesterol: 32 mg, Sodium: 160 mg, Potassium: 138 mg, Fiber: 1 g, Sugar: 3 g, Vitamin A: 135 IU, Vitamin C: 1 mg, Calcium: 62 mg, Iron: 1 mg

41. Chicken Jalfrezi

Chicken Jalfrezi is a popular Indian dish where succulent chicken is cooked in a fragrant spices and a tangy sauce until tender.

Serving: 4

Preparation time: 10 minutes

Ready time: 30 minutes

Ingredients:
- 500g chicken, cut into small cubes
- 1 onion, finely chopped
- 2 tsp garam masala
- 1 tsp coriander powder
- 1 tsp cumin powder
- 1 tsp chilli powder
- 2 red chillies, finely chopped
- 2 tomatoes, roughly chopped
- 2 tbsp tomato puree
- Salt to taste
- 2 garlic cloves, finely chopped
- 1-inch ginger, finely chopped
- 2 tbsp vegetable oil

Instructions:

1. Heat oil in a deep pan.
2. Add onion and sauté until lightly browned.
3. Add garlic and ginger and cook for a few seconds.
4. Add chicken and stir-fry for 3-4 minutes.
5. Add all the dry spices - garam masala, coriander powder, cumin powder, chilli powder and salt.
6. Stir in tomatoes and tomato puree and cook until the chicken is tender.
7. Add chillies and cook for a further 2 minutes.
8. Serve hot with rice or naan.

Nutrition information:
Serving size: 1/4 of the dish
Calories: 280
Fat: 15g
Protein: 17g
Carbohydrates: 18g

42. Key Lime Pie

Key Lime Pie is a classic and heavenly dessert that is a popular choice at many restaurants. Similar to a lemon or coconut custard, this dessert is made up of an egg custard filling set in a grilled or baked crust and is topped with meringue or whipped topping. It is the perfect balance of tart and sweet.
Serving: 8-10
Preparation time: 25-30 minutes
Ready time: 3-4 hours

Ingredients:
Crust:
• 1 ½ cups graham cracker crumbs
• 4 tablespoons (½ stick) unsalted butter, melted
Filling:
• 2 cups sweetened condensed milk
• 4 egg yolks
• ¾ cup key lime juice
• 1 teaspoon finely grated lime zest

Topping:
- 4 egg whites
- ¼ teaspoon cream of tartar
- ¾ cup granulated sugar

Instructions:

1. Prepare the Crust: Preheat the oven to 350°F. Coat a 9-inch pie plate with cooking spray. Put the graham cracker crumbs in the coated pie plate, and pour the melted butter over the crumbs. Mix well, and press the crumbs evenly over the bottom and up the sides of the pan. Bake for 8 minutes. Rotate the pan and bake for 6 minutes more. Remove the shell from the oven and let it cool.

2. Prepare the Filling: Whisk together the sweetened condensed milk, egg yolks, key lime juice, and lime zest until combined. Pour the filling into the cooled crust shell.

3. Bake for 12-15 minutes, until set. The center should still jiggle slightly when the pie is done. Remove from the oven and set aside on a wire rack.

4. Prepare the Topping: In a thermomixer, beat the egg whites and cream of tartar until soft peaks form. Gradually add the granulated sugar and increase the speed, beating until stiff peaks form.

5. Spread the meringue over the cooled filling, sealing it to the edges of the pre-baked crust to prevent shrinkage during baking.

6. Bake for 10-12 minutes, until the top of the bakes turns a golden-brown. Let cool completely before serving.

Nutrition information:
Calories: 275
Fat: 12.8g
Carbohydrate: 32.2g
Protein: 6.3g

43. Vegetable Samosas

Vegetable Samosas are a popular Indian snack made with potatoes, peas, and various spices, all encased in a flaky crispy pastry.
Serving: 6-8 persons
Preparation Time: 20 minutes

Ready Time: 30 minutes

Ingredients:
- 3 cups white all-purpose flour
- 2 tablespoons oil
- 1 teaspoon ghee
- A pinch of baking soda
- Salt, to taste
- Water, as required
- 2 potatoes, boiled, peeled, and mashed
- 1/2 cup green peas, boiled
- 1 teaspoon red chilli powder
- 1 teaspoon garam masala
- 2 tablespoons finely-chopped coriander leaves
- 2 tablespoons lemon juice
- Oil, for deep frying

Instructions:
1. In a bowl, mix together the flour, oil, ghee, baking soda, and salt.
2. Add water and knead into a soft dough and keep aside for 15 minutes.
3. In a large bowl, mix together mashed potatoes, green peas, red chilli powder, garam masala, coriander leaves, and lemon juice.
4. Divide the dough into 6-8 equal portions and roll into the cylindrical shape.
5. Cut the dough into equal lengths.
6. Take each strip and roll it into a cone-like shape.
7. Fill each cone with the potato-pea mixture and seal with a little water.
8. Heat the oil and deep fry the samosas until golden and crisp.
9. Serve hot with chutney.

Nutrition information:
- Calories: 270 kcal
- Carbohydrates: 33g
- Protein: 5g
- Fat: 14g
- Cholesterol: 0mg
- Sodium: 300mg

44. Sticky Ginger Cake

A delicious, moist, fluffy and spicy Sticky Ginger Cake, packed with incredible flavor and texture.
Serving: 8-10
Preparation Time: 10 minutes
Ready Time: 40 minutes

Ingredients:
- 1 1/2 cups all-purpose flour
- 3/4 cup dark brown sugar
- 1 teaspoon cinnamon
- 2 teaspoons ground ginger
- 2 teaspoons baking powder
- 1/2 teaspoon baking soda
- 3 tablespoons butter, melted
- 2 large eggs
- 2/3 cup plus 2 tablespoons mild molasses
- 6 tablespoons vegetable oil
- 2/3 cup buttermilk

Instructions:
1. Preheat oven to 350°F. Grease an 8x8-inch baking pan and line with parchment paper.
2. In a medium bowl, combine flour, sugar, cinnamon, ginger, baking powder and baking soda.
3. In a separate bowl, mix together the melted butter, eggs, molasses and vegetable oil.
4. Add the wet Ingredients to the dry Ingredients and mix until just combined.
5. Slowly add the buttermilk and mix until just combined.
6. Pour the batter into the prepared baking pan and spread it out evenly.
7. Bake for 35-40 minutes, or until a toothpick comes out clean.
8. Let the cake cool completely before slicing and serving.

Nutrition information: Per Serving: Calories 315, Fat 14 g, Saturated fat 5 g, Cholesterol 52 mg, Sodium 134 mg, Carbohydrates 43 g, Fiber 1 g, Sugar 27 g, Protein 5 g

45. Chicken Biryani Stuffed Peppers

Spice up your next dinner with this delicious Chicken Biryani Stuffed Peppers recipe! Perfect for a weeknight meal, these stuffed peppers are loaded with flavor and sure to please the whole family.

Serving: 6
Preparation Time: 25 minutes
Ready Time: 1 hour

Ingredients:
- 3 bell peppers, halved, seeded
- 2 cups cooked basmati rice
- 2 tablespoons vegetable oil
- 1 small onion, diced
- 1 clove garlic, minced
- 1 teaspoon grated ginger
- 1 teaspoon cumin
- 1 teaspoon coriander
- 1 teaspoon garam masala
- 1/2 teaspoon turmeric
- 1/4 teaspoon cayenne pepper
- 2 cups cooked, shredded chicken
- 1/2 cup frozen peas
- Salt and pepper, to taste
- 1/4 cup chopped cilantro

Instructions:
1. Preheat oven to 375 degrees F.
2. Place the peppers on a baking sheet and drizzle with some oil. Bake for 20 minutes.
3. Heat the remaining oil in a large skillet over medium heat. Add the onion and cook until softened, about 5 minutes.
4. Add the garlic, ginger, cumin, coriander, garam masala, turmeric, and cayenne pepper. Cook, stirring, for 1 minute.
5. Add the cooked rice, chicken, and peas to the skillet. Stir to combine and season with salt and pepper.
6. Divide the mixture among the peppers and bake for an additional 20 minutes.
7. Garnish with fresh cilantro and serve.

Nutrition information:
- Calorie: 280
- Protein: 19g
- Fat: 8g
- Carbohydrates: 35g
- Fiber: 3g
- Sugar: 5g
- Sodium: 890mg

46. Chocolate Eclairs

Chocolate Eclairs are a delicious and classic French pastry made with choux pastry filled with a creamy custard and topped with a chocolate glaze.
Serving: 4
Preparation time: 30 minutes
Ready time: 1 hour and 20 minutes

Ingredients:
-¼ cup unsalted butter
-½ teaspoon sugar
-¾ cup all-purpose flour
-2 eggs
-1 cup heavy cream
-4 tablespoons granulated sugar
-1 teaspoon vanilla extract
-4 ounces bittersweet chocolate

Instructions:
1. Preheat oven to 375°F.
2. In a medium saucepan over medium heat, melt butter. Add sugar and stir until dissolved. Add flour, stirring until a paste forms.
3. Add eggs, one at a time, stirring until completely incorporated.
4. Transfer dough to a pastry bag with a large star tip. Pipe 4-inch strips onto a parchment-lined baking sheet.
5. Bake for 20 minutes, or until golden brown.
6. In a medium bowl, whisk together heavy cream, sugar, and vanilla extract until smooth.

7. Fill cooled eclairs with cream filling and top with melted chocolate.

Nutrition information:
Calories: 250, Total Fat: 16g, Saturated Fat: 10g, Cholesterol: 75mg, Sodium: 35mg, Carbohydrates: 21g, Fiber: 1g, Sugars: 10g, Protein: 5g

47. Lamb Rogan Josh

Lamb Rogan Josh is a delectable dish from Northern India full of flavor and warm spices.
Serving: 6 servings
Preparation time: 15 minutes
Ready time: 60 minutes

Ingredients:
- 3 tablespoons vegetable oil
- 2 large onions, chopped
- 2 cloves garlic, minced
- 2 teaspoons ground coriander
- 2 teaspoons ground cumin
- 1 teaspoon ground ginger
- 1 teaspoon ground turmeric
- 1 teaspoon ground cayenne pepper
- 2 teaspoons salt
- 1 teaspoon ground black pepper
- 2 pounds boneless lamb, cubed
- 2 cups tomato sauce
- 1 cup plain yogurt
- 1/2 cup chopped fresh cilantro

Instructions:
1. Heat oil in a large skillet over medium-high heat.
2. Add onions and garlic and cook until lightly browned.
3. Stir in coriander, cumin, ginger, turmeric, cayenne pepper, salt, and pepper.
4. Add the lamb cubes and cook until lightly browned on all sides.
5. Add tomato sauce and bring to a simmer.

6. Reduce heat to low and simmer for 30 minutes or until the lamb is tender.

7. Stir in the yogurt and cilantro and simmer for an additional 5 minutes.

Nutrition information: Calories: 331, Fat: 16g, Cholesterol: 68mg, Sodium: 928mg, Carbohydrates: 20g, Protein: 26g, Potassium: 673mg, Fiber: 2g.

48. Mango and Coconut Rice

Mango and Coconut Rice is a warm and flavorful dish perfect for a quick weeknight dinner. It is made with creamy coconut milk and fragrant mango for the perfect combination of sweetness and savoriness.
Serving: 6-8
Preparation time: 10 minutes
Ready time: 30 minutes

Ingredients:
- 2 cups basmati rice
- 2 cups of coconut milk
- 2 mangoes, cubed
- 1 teaspoon coriander powder
- 2 tablespoons olive oil
- 1/2 teaspoon turmeric powder
- Salt and pepper to taste

Instructions:
1. Begin by cooking the rice with a 2:1 water-rice mixture.
2. In a separate pot, heat the olive oil on low heat and add the coriander powder, turmeric powder, salt, and pepper. Add the cubed mangoes and cook until tender.
3. Once the rice is done cooking,, add the coconut milk and the mango mixture and stir to combine.
4. Allow the mixture to simmer until the coconut milk is completely absorbed, stirring occasionally.

Nutrition information: Per serving (based on 8 servings): Calories: 303, Fat: 12 g, Saturated fat: 7 g, Carbohydrates: 44 g, Sugar: 6.2 g, Fiber: 2.7 g, Protein: 4.5 g

49. Chicken Satay Skewers

This easy chicken satay skewers recipe uses a simple marinade to infuse the chicken with flavor, and is perfect for an appetizer or main dish that's ready in under an hour.
Serving: 4
Preparation time: 10 minutes
Ready time: 55 minutes

Ingredients:
- 8 wooden skewers, soaked in water for 30 minutes
- 1/2 cup coconut milk
- 1/2 red onion, roughly chopped
- 2 garlic cloves, peeled
- 1 teaspoon fresh ginger, peeled and finely chopped
- 2 tablespoons freshly squeezed lime juice
- 2 tablespoons brown sugar
- 2 tablespoons fish sauce
- 1 teaspoon ground coriander
- 1 teaspoon chili powder
- 1/2 teaspoon ground turmeric
- 1/2 teaspoon ground cumin
- 1 lb skinless, boneless chicken breasts, cut into 1-inch cubes

Instructions:
1. In a blender, combine the coconut milk, red onion, garlic, ginger, lime juice, brown sugar, fish sauce, coriander, chili powder, turmeric, and cumin. Blend until smooth and set aside.
2. In a bowl, combine the chicken and the marinade. Mix well and let marinate in the refrigerator for from 30 minutes to overnight.
3. On each skewer, thread 5-6 cubes of chicken.
4. Preheat a grill to medium high heat and oil the grate to prevent sticking.

5. Place skewers on the hot grill and cook for 10-12 minutes, flipping every few minutes, until the chicken is cooked through and no longer pink in the center.

Nutrition information: 227 calories; 10.3 grams of fat; 15.2 grams of carbohydrates; 14.5 grams of protein.

50. Vanilla Cupcakes

Vanilla Cupcakes are a classic treat that can be enjoyed as dessert, a snack, or for any special occasion. This incredibly simple recipe requires a few everyday Ingredients that will create a soft, buttery, and lightly sweetened cupcake that will have you coming back for more.
Serving: Makes 24 cupcakes
Preparation Time: 15 minutes
Ready Time: 25 minutes

Ingredients:
• 3 1/2 cups all-purpose flour
• 2 teaspoons baking powder
• 1 teaspoon baking soda
• 3/4 teaspoon salt
• 1 1/2 cups (3 sticks) unsalted butter, softened
• 2 cups granulated sugar
• 4 large eggs
• 2 teaspoons vanilla extract
• 1 1/2 cups buttermilk

Instructions:
1. Preheat oven to 350°F. Line a 12-cup muffin tin with paper liners.
2. In a medium bowl, whisk together the flour, baking powder, baking soda, and salt.
3. Using a stand mixer, beat the butter and sugar together until light and fluffy. Beat in the eggs, one at a time, then add the vanilla extract.
4. With the mixer on low, slowly add the dry Ingredients, alternating with the buttermilk, and beat until just incorporated.

5. Divide the batter among the prepared muffin cups. Bake 20–25 minutes, or until a toothpick inserted into the center of a cupcake comes out clean.

6. Cool the cupcakes in the pan for 10 minutes, then transfer to a wire rack to cool completely before serving.

Nutrition information
Calories – 230
Total Fat – 11 g
Saturated Fat – 7 g
Cholesterol – 50 mg
Sodium – 210 mg
Total Carbohydrate – 29 g
Protein – 2 g

51. Vegetable Spring Rolls

Vegetable Spring Rolls are a delicious and crunchy appetizer or snack which is full of fresh vegetables. These crispy rolls can be quickly and easily made with a few simple Ingredients.
Serving - Makes 8-10 rolls
Preparation Time - 10 minutes
Ready Time - 15 minutes

Ingredients:
- 1 large carrot, julienned
- 4 ounces red cabbage, julienned
- 1/4 red bell pepper, julienned
- 2 drop green onions, sliced
- 1 1/2 tablespoons soy sauce
- 1 tablespoon sesame oil
- 8-10 spring roll wrappers

Instructions:
1. Mix together the carrots, cabbage, bell pepper, and green onions in a medium-sized bowl.
2. Add in the soy sauce and sesame oil and mix until everything is evenly combined.

3. Place a spring roll wrapper on a clean surface or cutting board.
4. Put a heaping tablespoonful of the vegetable filling onto the center of the wrapper.
5. Fold in the sides of the wrapper to cover the filling and roll the wrapper up, making sure to seal the edges.
6. Heat a large non-stick skillet or wok over medium-high heat.
7. Add a tablespoon of oil to the skillet or wok and swirl it around.
8. Arrange the Vegetable Spring Rolls in the skillet or wok, making sure they are not touching.
9. Cook for about 2-3 minutes each side, flipping half way through. They should be golden brown and crispy when done.
10. Serve while hot. Enjoy!

Nutrition information -
Calories: 78
Protein: 1.6 g
Fat: 2 g
Carbohydrates: 13.1 g
Sodium: 148 mg

52. Salted Caramel Brownies

Check out these soft and chocolatey Salted Caramel Brownies! This recipe combines crunchy salt with sweet caramel to delight your taste buds.
Serving: Makes 16 brownies.
Preparation Time: 30 minutes.
Ready Time: 45 minutes.

Ingredients:
• 2 tablespoons of butter or margarine
• 1/2 cup of sugar
• 2 tablespoons of unsweetened cocoa powder
• 1/4 teaspoon of salt
• 2 eggs
• 1/2 cup of all-purpose flour
• 1/2 teaspoon of baking powder
• 1/2 cup of caramel sauce

• 2 tablespoons of coarse sea salt

Instructions:
1. Preheat oven to 350°F and grease an 8-inch-square baking pan.
2. In a medium-size bowl, cream together butter and sugar until light and fluffy. Add cocoa powder, salt, and eggs and beat together until combined.
3. In a separate bowl, combine flour and baking powder. Gradually add this mixture to the butter-sugar mixture, stirring until combined.
4. Spread the batter evenly in the prepared baking pan. Drizzle with caramel sauce and lightly sprinkle with coarse sea salt.
5. Bake for 20-25 minutes, or until a toothpick inserted into the center comes out clean.
6. Let cool before serving.

Nutrition information: Per brownie: 138 calories; 6g fat; 18g carbohydrates; 2g protein.

53. Chicken Tandoori Burgers

This delicious and spicy chicken tandoori burger will make your taste buds dance with delight. This quick and easy meal is packed with plenty of flavour, and sure to please even the most discerning of eaters.
Serving: Serves up to 4 people
Preparation time: 15 minutes
Ready time: 25 minutes

Ingredients:
- 4 chicken mince patties
- 2 tablespoons tandoori paste
- 2 tablespoons olive oil
- 4 fresh hamburger buns
- 1/2 red onion, finely diced
- 1 tomato, sliced
- 1/4 cup greek yoghurt
- 2 tablespoons mango chutney
- 2 tablespoons fresh coriander, finely chopped
- Salt and pepper, to taste

Instructions:
1. Preheat the oven to 200C.
2. In a bowl, mix together the chicken mince, tandoori paste, olive oil and a pinch of salt and pepper. Form into 4 patties.
3. Place the patties on a lined baking tray and into the preheated oven. Bake for 15 minutes, then set aside to cool.
4. To assemble the burgers, spread the greek yoghurt on the bottom buns, followed by the red onion, tomato slices, chicken patties and mango chutney. Top with the remaining buns.
5. Serve with a sprinkle of fresh coriander and enjoy!

Nutrition information:
Calories: 350 kcal
Protein: 19g
Fat: 10g
Carbs: 34g

54. Eton Mess

Eton Mess is a classic British dessert made with chunks of meringue, mixed with fresh cream and topped with seasonal fruits of your choice. This light, low fat, and no-bake dessert is delicious and easy to make.
Serving
Makes 4 large servings.
Preparation time: 10 minutes.
Ready Time
30 minutes.

Ingredients:
- 4 large meringues, crushed
- 340g/12oz fresh strawberries, hulled and sliced
- 300ml/10floz whipping cream, lightly whipped
- 2 tablespoons icing sugar

Instructions:
1. Place the meringues in a bowl and mix with the cream and icing sugar.

2. Gently fold in the strawberries and transfer the mixture to individual glasses.

3. Garnish with extra strawberries and serve chilled.

Nutrition information
Per serving: Calories 311, Fat 20.3g, Saturated Fat 12.5g, Cholesterol 62.5mg, Carbohydrates 28.4g, Protein 4.5g

55. Aloo Tikki

Aloo Tikki is a popular Indian snack made of mashed potatoes and a blend of spices. It is eaten plain, or served with chutneys or sauces.
Serving: 4
Preparation Time: 10 minutes
Ready Time: 25 minutes

Ingredients:
• 2 large potatoes
• 2 tablespoons finely chopped onion
• 2 tablespoons oil
• 1 teaspoon finely chopped fresh ginger
• ½ green chili, finely chopped
• 1 teaspoon coriander powder
• 1 teaspoon cumin powder
• ½ teaspoon garam masala
• 2 tablespoons coriander leaves, finely chopped
• Salt to taste
• 3 tablespoons plain bread crumbs
• Oil for shallow frying

Instructions:
1. Place the potatoes in a large pan, cover with water and bring to a boil. Cook until soft. Drain the potatoes and leave to cool for 10 minutes. Peel and mash them in a bowl.

2. Heat the oil in a pan on a medium heat. Add the onion, ginger and chili and fry for 2 minutes. Add the coriander, cumin and garam masala and continue to fry for 1 more minute.

3. Remove the pan from the heat and add the coriander leaves, mashed potatoes, salt and bread crumbs. Mix well to combine.

4. To form the tikkis, take 2 tablespoons of the mixture and shape into a patty. Repeat with the remaining mixture.

5. Heat oil in a pan for shallow frying. Place the tikkis in the pan, in batches. Fry for 3 minutes on each side until golden brown.

Nutrition information:

Calories: 176.6 Carbohydrates: 24.4g Protein: 4.1g Fat: 6.9g Cholesterol: 0mg Sodium: 105.6mg Potassium: 463.5mg Fiber: 3.6g Sugar: 1.5g Vitamin A: 115.8IU Vitamin C: 13.7mg Calcium: 44.9mg Iron: 2.1mg

56. Raspberry and White Chocolate Muffins

There's nothing like homemade raspberry and white chocolate muffins to make your day just a little sweeter. With their delicious combination of tartness from the raspberries and sweetness from the white chocolate chips, these muffins can be served as breakfast, as dessert, or as an indulgent snack!

Serving: Makes 6 muffins

Preparation time: 10 minutes

Ready time: 25 minutes

Ingredients:

- 1 ½ cups Self-Rising Flour
- ½ cup Sugar
- ¼ teaspoon Salt
- 6 tablespoons Butter, melted
- ½ cup Milk
- 1 Egg
- 1 cup fresh Raspberries
- ½ cup White Chocolate Chips

Instructions:

1. Preheat the oven to 400°F and line a muffin tin with 6 liners.

2. In a large bowl, mix together the flour, sugar, and salt.

3. In a separate bowl, whisk together the butter, milk, and egg.

4. Pour the wet Ingredients into the dry Ingredients and mix until just combined.
5. Fold in the raspberries and white chocolate chips.
6. Divide the batter evenly among the muffin liners.
7. Bake for 20-25 minutes until the tops of the muffins are golden brown.
8. Serve warm and enjoy!

Nutrition information: Per 1 muffin: Calories – 315, Total Fat – 15 g, Carbs – 37 g, Protein – 4 g

57. Lamb Samosas

Lamb samosas are traditional fried pastries packed with a savory lamb and vegetable filling. These flaky, delicious morsels of flavor are perfect for appetizers or as a crispy snack.
Serving: This recipe makes 12 samosas.
Preparation time: 70 minutes
Ready Time: 90 minutes

Ingredients:
-1 pound ground lamb
-1 onion , diced
-1/2 bell pepper , diced
-2 cloves garlic, minced
-2 inch piece of ginger, minced
-2 tablespoons curry powder
-1 teaspoon cumin
-1 teaspoon coriander powder
-1/4 teaspoon turmeric powder
-1/4 teaspoon red chili powder
-1/2 teaspoon garam masala
- 1/2 cup peas
-2 tablespoons sunflower oil
-1/2 cup cilantro leaves, chopped
-Salt, to taste
-24 wonton wrappers
-Oil, for frying

Instructions:

1. Heat the sunflower oil in a large skillet over medium-high heat.
2. Add the lamb and onion to the skillet and cook, stirring often, until the lamb is cooked through and the onion is beginning to soften, about 6 minutes.
3. Add the bell pepper, garlic, and ginger to the skillet and continue to cook, stirring often, until the bell pepper is softened, about 4 minutes.
4. Mix in the curry powder, cumin, coriander powder, turmeric, red chili powder and garam masala and stir until combined.
5. Stir in the peas and cilantro and season to taste with salt. Remove the skillet from heat and set aside to cool.
6. Place one wonton wrapper on the work surface and lightly wet the edges with a dab of water.
7. Place 1 tablespoon of the meat mixture in the center of the wrapper.
8. Fold the wrapper over and press the edges with a fork to seal.
9. Continue to fill the rest of the wrappers.
10. Heat oil for frying in a medium-sized saucepan over medium-high heat.
11. Working in batches, fry the samosas until golden brown and cooked through, about 4 minutes.
12. Transfer to a plate lined with paper towels to drain any excess oil.

Nutrition information

Serving size: 2 samosas; Calories: 169kcal; Carbohydrates: 15g; Protein: 9g; Fat: 8g; Saturated Fat: 2g; Cholesterol: 20mg; Sodium: 187mg; Potassium: 121mg; Fiber: 1g; Sugar: 1g; Vitamin A: 116IU; Vitamin C: 11mg; Calcium: 21mg; Iron: 1mg

58. Lemon Curd Tart

With a buttery crust and sweet-tart lemon curd, this Lemon Curd Tart is a classic summertime dessert that is sure to please.
Serving: 8-10
Preparation Time: 15 minutes
Ready Time: 2 hours

Ingredients:

-1/2 cup (1 stick) butter, melted
-1/2 cup granulated sugar
-1/2 teaspoon vanilla extract
-1 large egg
-1 1/2 cups all-purpose flour
-3/4 teaspoon baking powder
-1/8 teaspoon salt
-2/3 cup prepared lemon curd

Instructions:

1. Preheat oven to 350°F. Grease and flour a 9-inch tart pan and set aside.
2. In a medium-size bowl, combine melted butter, sugar, and vanilla extract. Beat in egg until combined.
3. In a separate bowl, mix together flour, baking powder, and salt.
4. Slowly add dry Ingredients to wet and mix until just combined. Do not overmix.
5. Press dough evenly into prepared tart pan.
6. Spread lemon curd over dough.
7. Bake for 25-30 minutes, or until golden brown.
8. Allow to cool completely before serving.

Nutrition information:

Serving size: 1 slice (1/10 of tart). Calories: 250, Fat: 12g, Saturated Fat: 7g, Cholesterol: 45mg, Sodium: 125mg, Carbohydrates: 33g, Fiber: 1g, Sugar: 14g, Protein: 2g.

59. Chicken Biryani Stuffed Bell Peppers

Enjoy a delicious meal of delectable and nutritious Chicken Biryani Stuffed Bell Peppers. This meal is full of flavorful Indian spices and tender chicken, making it a wonderful dish to share with family and friends.
Serving: Makes 4-6 Servings
Preparation Time: 25 minutes
Ready Time: 1 hour

Ingredients:

-4-6 large bell peppers
-1 ½ cups cooked basmati rice
-2 cloves garlic, minced
-2 teaspoons ground ginger
-1 medium onion, finely chopped
-1 teaspoon garam masala
-1 ½ cups cooked chicken, diced
-⅓ cup plain yogurt
-⅓ cup raisins
-1 tablespoon olive oil
-Salt and pepper to taste

Instructions:

1. Preheat oven to 375 degrees F and cut the top off the bell peppers. Discard tops and scoop out seeds and ribs.
2. Heat olive oil in a medium skillet over medium-high heat. Add onion and garlic and cook until softened, about 5 minutes.
3. Add ginger, garam masala, salt, and pepper and cook an additional 1-2 minutes. Remove from heat.
4. In a large bowl, combine cooked rice, cooked chicken, yogurt, raisins, and cooked onion-garlic mixture. Mix well to combine.
5. Place bell peppers in a baking dish and stuff with prepared biryani mixture.
6. Bake for 40-45 minutes or until peppers are tender.

Nutrition information:

Per Serving: Calories 439, Total Fat 11.5 g, Saturated Fat 2.5 g, Cholesterol 50 mg, Sodium 181.5 mg, Total Carbohydrates 51.9 g, Dietary Fiber 6.3 g, Protein 28.6 g

60. Chocolate Fudge Cake

Indulge your sweet tooth with this classic and delicious Chocolate Fudge Cake. The cake is soft, moist, and rich with a delicious layers of chocolate fudge.
Serving: 6-8
Preparation Time: 15 minutes
Ready Time: 1 hour

Ingredients:
- 2 ½ cups All-Purpose Flour
- 2 cups Sugar
- 2/3 cup Cocoa Powder
- ½ teaspoon Baking Soda
- ½ teaspoon Salt
- 1 cup Buttermilk
- ½ cup Vegetable Oil
- 2 large Eggs
- 2 teaspoons Vanilla Extract
- 1 teaspoon Instant Coffee
- Fudge Frosting

Instructions:
1. Preheat your oven to 350°F and lightly grease a 9×13" baking dish.
2. In a medium bowl, whisk together the all-purpose flour, sugar, cocoa powder, baking soda, and salt.
3. In a separate bowl, mix together the buttermilk, oil, eggs, vanilla extract, and instant coffee.
4. Slowly add the wet Ingredients to the dry Ingredients and mix together until everything is just combined.
5. Pour the batter into the baking dish and bake for 40 minutes.
6. Allow the cake to cool completely before frosting with the fudge frosting.
7. Enjoy!

Nutrition information: Per Serving (1/8th of cake): 368 Calories, 9g Fat, 64g Carbohydrates, 2g Fiber, 6g Protein

61. Lamb Chops with Mint Sauce

Lamb Chops with Mint Sauce is a flavorful and delicious dish made with juicy lamb chops, a zesty mint sauce, and other seasonings. Serve it as a entrée or as a wonderful addition to any meal.
Serving: 4
Preparation Time: 10 minutes
Ready Time: 30 minutes

Ingredients:
- 4 lamb chops
- 2 tablespoons olive oil
- 1 teaspoon freshly ground black pepper
- 2 tablespoons fresh mint, finely chopped
- 1 tablespoon mustard
- 2 tablespoons butter
- Juice of ½ a lemon

Instructions:
1. Preheat your oven to 400°F.
2. In a large bowl, combine the olive oil, pepper, mint, mustard, and lemon juice.
3. Place the lamb chops in the bowl and coat them thoroughly in the marinade.
4. Place the lamb chops in a shallow baking dish and bake for 18-20 minutes, or until the chops are cooked through.
5. Melt the butter in a saucepan over medium heat.
6. Add in the remaining marinade and stir to combine. Simmer the sauce until it thickens slightly.
7. Serve the cooked lamb chops with the warm mint sauce.

Nutrition information: Calories: 369, Carbs: 1g, Protein: 19g, Fat: 32g, Cholesterol: 77mg, Sodium: 250mg, Sugar: 0.3g.

62. Mango and Passion Fruit Pavlova

Mango and passion fruit Pavlova is an exquisite, light and fluffy meringue-based dessert. With juicy mango and tangy passion fruit, it is a heavenly combination topped with sweet whipped cream.
Serving: 8
Preparation time: 25 minutes
Ready time: 2 hours

Ingredients:
- 6 egg whites
- 2¼ cups superfine sugar

- 3 tsp cornstarch
- 2 tsp white wine vinegar
- 2 passion fruits
- 1 ripe mango
- whipped cream

Instructions:
1. Preheat the oven to 300oF and line a baking tray with parchment paper.
2. Using an electric mixer, beat the egg whites until it holds stiff peaks.
3. Gradually add the sugar to the egg whites, beating until it is glossy.
4. Add in the cornstarch and vinegar and mix until fully incorporated.
5. Pour the meringue mixture onto the parchment paper and spread it into an even circle, about 9-10 inches in diameter.
6. Bake the Pavlova base for 1 hour 30 minutes. Once baked, turn off the oven and leave the Pavlova inside to cool.
7. Slice the mango and scoop out the flesh from the passion fruits.
8. When the Pavlova is cool, pile the Passion fruit and mango on top.
9. Top generously with whipped cream.

Nutrition information:
Calories: 242kcal
Carbohydrates: 45g
Protein: 3g
Fats: 5g
Saturated Fats: 4g
Sugar: 42g
Sodium: 35mg

63. Spinach and Feta Samosas

Spinach and Feta Samosas are a delicious type of Indian appetizer, filled with the savory combination of spinach, feta, and spices. They are perfect for any occasion, from an evening get-together to a large family gathering.
Serving: Makes 16 samosas
Preparation Time: 25 minutes
Ready Time: 25 minutes

Ingredients:

- 2 tablespoons vegetable oil
- 2 cups finely chopped spinach
- 1/2 cup crumbled feta cheese
- 2 tablespoons finely grated onion
- 2 tablespoons minced fresh ginger
- 1 teaspoon ground cumin
- 1 teaspoon ground coriander
- 1/2 teaspoon ground turmeric
- 1/4 teaspoon cayenne pepper
- 2 tablespoons chopped fresh cilantro
- 16 (4-inch) round prepared frozen samosa wrappers
- All-purpose flour for rolling
- Oil for deep-frying

Instructions:

1. Heat the oil in a large saucepan over medium heat. Add the spinach and cook, stirring often, until the spinach has wilted, about 5 minutes.
2. Add the feta cheese, onion, ginger, cumin, coriander, turmeric, and cayenne pepper and cook, stirring often, until fragrant, about 1 minute. Stir in the cilantro and remove from the heat. Set aside.
3. Place the samosa wrappers on a work surface. Dust lightly with flour. Cut each wrapper in half, making 32 halves total.
4. Working with one wrapper half at a time, moisten the edges with water. Place about 1 tablespoon of the spinach filling on the wrapper and fold the wrapper over the filling to make a triangle shape. Pinch the edges together to seal. Repeat with the remaining wrapper halves and filling.
5. Heat the oil in a deep fryer to 375 degrees F. Deep-fry the samosas in batches until golden brown, about 2 to 3 minutes per batch. Drain on paper towels. Serve warm.

Nutrition information: Nutrition information per serving (1 samosa): 80 calories, 5g fat, 1g saturated fat, 20mg cholesterol, 120mg sodium, 6g carbohydrates, 1g fiber, 1g sugar, 3g protein.

64. Caramel Apple Crumble

This Caramel Apple Crumble is a sweet and easy-to-make dessert perfect for any occasion. Rich in flavor and loaded with fresh apples, caramel, and a crunchy topping, this masterpiece is sure to satisfy any sweet tooth.
Serving: 8
Preparation Time: 15 minutes
Ready Time: 45 minutes

Ingredients:
• 6-7 apples (any variety) peeled, cored, and chopped
• 1/2 cup caramel sauce
• 1/2 cup butter, softened
• 1/2 cup brown sugar
• 1 teaspoon ground cinnamon
• 1 cup all-purpose flour
• 3/4 cup rolled oats

Instructions:
1. Preheat oven to 350 degrees F.
2. Grease an 8-inch square baking dish.
3. Place the chopped apples in the baking dish and evenly sprinkle caramel sauce over it.
4. In a separate bowl, mix together the butter, brown sugar, cinnamon, flour, and oats until it is a crumbly texture.
5. Sprinkle the crumble mixture over the apples.
6. Bake for about 35-45 minutes or until golden brown.
7. Let cool slightly before serving.

Nutrition information:
Calories: 287g, Total Fat: 14g, Cholesterol: 31mg, Sodium: 110mg, Carbohydrates: 37g, Protein: 2g.

65. Chicken Tikka Skewers

Chicken Tikka Skewers is an easy to make Indian dish, consisting of marinated cubes of chicken threaded onto skewers and grilled.
Serving: Up to 4

Preparation Time: 30 minutes
Ready Time: 1 hour

Ingredients:
- 1 pound boneless skinless organic chicken breast, cubed
- 1 teaspoon garam masala
- 1 teaspoon curry powder
- 1 teaspoon lemon juice
- 2 teaspoons olive oil
- ½ teaspoon sea salt
- 1 garlic clove, minced
- 2 tablespoons plain yogurt

Instructions:
1. In a bowl, combine the garam masala, curry powder, lemon juice, olive oil, sea salt and garlic.
2. Add the cubed chicken and stir to combine.
3. Cover the bowl and refrigerate so the chicken can marinate for up to an hour.
4. Pre-heat the grill to medium-high heat.
5. Once the grill is hot, thread the chicken onto skewers.
6. Cook the chicken skewers for 4-5 minutes per side or until the chicken is cooked through.
7. Serve with a side of plain yogurt.

Nutrition information:
Calories per serving: 215
Protein per serving: 24g
Fat per serving: 6g
Carbohydrates per serving: 4g

66. Pistachio and Rosewater Cake

This moist and flavorful Pistachio and Rosewater Cake is a delicious and unique treat that's perfect for an afternoon snack.
Serving: Makes one 9-inch cake; serves 8-10
Preparation Time: 15 mins
Ready Time: 50 minutes

Ingredients:
- 2 cups all-purpose flour
- 1 teaspoon baking powder
- 1/2 teaspoon baking soda
- 1/4 teaspoon fine sea salt
- 2/3 cup granulated sugar
- 1/2 cup pistachios, coarsely chopped
- 3/4 cup plain Greek yogurt
- 1/2 cup canola oil
- 1/4 cup rosewater
- zest of 1 lemon
- 2 large eggs
- 2 tablespoons rose petals

Instructions:
1. Preheat oven to 350 degrees F. Grease and line a 9-inch round cake pan with parchment paper.
2. In a large bowl, whisk together the flour, baking powder, baking soda, and salt. In a medium bowl, whisk together the sugar, pistachios, yogurt, oil, rosewater, and lemon zest.
3. Beat the eggs into the yogurt mixture until well combined. Slowly add the dry Ingredients, mixing until just combined.
4. Scrape the batter into the prepared baking pan. Sprinkle the rose petals on top.
5. Bake for 35-40 minutes, or until the top is golden brown and a toothpick inserted into the center of the cake comes out clean.
6. Allow cake to cool in the pan for 15 minutes before running a knife around the edges to loosen it. Carefully turn out onto a platter and cool completely.

Nutrition information: Per serving (1/10 of cake): 200 calories, 11 g total fat (1 g saturated fat), 24 g carbohydrate, 3 g protein, 1 g dietary fiber, 145 mg sodium.

67. Paneer Tikka

Paneer Tikka is a delicious Indian dish that is full of flavor and spices. It is made with paneer (an Indian cheese), vegetables, and a flavorful mix of spices. It is easy to prepare and perfect for sharing with friends and family.

Serving: 4
Preparation time: 10 minutes
Ready time: 25 minutes

Ingredients:
- 1 pound paneer (Indian cheese), cubed
- 2 tablespoons lemon juice
- 2 tablespoons oil
- 1 tablespoon garlic paste
- 1 tablespoon ginger paste
- 1 teaspoon ground cumin
- 1 teaspoon ground coriander
- 1 teaspoon garam masala
- 1 teaspoon chaat masala
- 1/2 teaspoon Kashmiri chili powder
- 1/2 teaspoon turmeric
- 1/4 teaspoon cayenne pepper
- 1 bell pepper, diced
- 1 onion, diced
- 1/2 cup plain yogurt

Instructions:
1. In a large bowl, combine the cubed paneer, lemon juice, oil, garlic paste, ginger paste, cumin, coriander, garam masala, chaat masala, chili powder, turmeric, and cayenne pepper. Mix until all the Ingredients are fully incorporated.
2. Preheat the oven to 475°F.
3. Place the seasoned paneer cubes into a baking dish.
4. Add the diced bell pepper and onion to the pan.
5. Pour the yogurt over the top and mix until everything is evenly coated.
6. Bake in the preheated oven for 15 minutes.
7. Take the baking dish out of the oven and broil for an additional 5 minutes.
8. Serve and enjoy.

Nutrition information:

- Calories: 200 kcal
- Carbohydrates: 8 g
- Protein: 13 g
- Fat: 10 g
- Sodium: 229 mg
- Potassium: 265 mg
- Fiber: 2 g
- Sugar: 5 g
- Vitamin A: 330 IU
- Vitamin C: 41.2 mg
- Calcium: 200 mg
- Iron: 0.8 mg

68. Coconut Macaroons

Coconut Macaroons are traditional small cakes or cookies made with shredded coconut, held together by egg whites and sugar. They are a popular dessert or snack in many countries.
Serving: Makes 24
Preparation Time: 15 minutes
Ready Time: 45 minutes

Ingredients:
- 2 egg whites
- 2/3 cup granulated white sugar
- 1/4 teaspoon salt
- 21/2 cups sweetened flaked coconut

Instructions:
1. Preheat oven to 350°F (175°C). Line two baking sheets with parchment paper.
2. In a large bowl, beat egg whites till foamy. Gradually beat in the sugar and salt, and continue beating until soft peaks form when beaters are lifted.
3. Gradually fold in the coconut until combined.
4. Drop by spoonfuls onto the prepared baking sheets. Place the baking sheets in the preheated oven and immediately turn the oven temperature down to 325°F (165°C).

5. Bake for 25 to 30 minutes, or until the tops are lightly browned. Place the baking sheets on cooling racks to cool.

Nutrition information:
- Calories: 102
- Fat: 6.5g
- Carbohydrates: 11g
- Protein: 1.5g

69. Chicken Katsu Curry

Chicken Katsu Curry is a delicious and flavorful Japanese dish that features breaded fried chicken cutlets served with curry sauce over steamed white rice.
Serving: 4
Preparation time: 10 minutes
Ready time: 30 minutes

Ingredients:
- 4 Skinless and boneless chicken breasts
- 1 cup all-purpose flour
- ¼ teaspoon ground black pepper
- 4 large eggs
- 2 cups breadcrumbs
- Vegetable oil, for frying
- 2 tablespoons butter
- 1 Onion, finely chopped
- 2 cloves garlic, minced
- 1 tablespoon fresh ginger, grated
- 2 tablespoons all-purpose flour
- 1 1/2 cups chicken broth
- 3 tablespoons honey
- 1 1/2 tablespoons apple cider vinegar
- 1 tablespoon savory curry powder
- 2 teaspoons garlic powder
- 1 teaspoon smoked paprika
- 1 teaspoon ground turmeric
- 2 teaspoons salt

• 1 cup cooked white rice

Instructions:
1. Preheat oven to 375°F.
2. Pound chicken breasts to ½ inch thick and cut into 4 equal portions.
3. In a shallow dish, add flour, black pepper, and salt. Mix until blended.
4. In a different shallow dish, crack eggs and beat until blended.
5. In a third shallow dish, spread the breadcrumbs.
6. Dip chicken portions into the flour, then the eggs, and finally into the breadcrumbs.
7. In a large skillet, heat 1 inch of vegetable oil over medium heat.
8. Fry the chicken until golden brown on each side, about 3 minutes per side.
9. Place the chicken on a baking sheet and bake for 20 minutes, or until the chicken is cooked through.
10. In a large saucepan, melt the butter over medium heat.
11. Add the onions, garlic, and ginger, and cook until the onions are softened.
12. Add the flour and stir for 1 minute.
13. Add the chicken broth, honey, apple cider vinegar, curry powder, garlic powder, smoked paprika, turmeric, and salt.
14. Stir until the sauce thickens, about 5 minutes.
15. Serve the chicken over a bed of white rice with curry sauce over top.

Nutrition information:
• Calories: 566
• Protein: 39g
• Fat: 25g
• Carbohydrates: 45g
• Sodium: 1227mg

70. Raspberry Swirl Cheesecake

Try this delicious raspberry swirl cheesecake recipe for your next special occasion or just for a treat! It is a creamy cheesecake filled with a sweet raspberry sauce and a buttery graham cracker crust.
Serving: 8
Preparation time: 20 minutes

Ready time: 2 hours

Ingredients:
- 2 cups graham cracker crumbs
- 1/3 cup melted butter
- 2 tablespoons sugar
- 16 ounces cream cheese, softened
- 1 cup sugar
- 2 eggs
- 2 teaspoons vanilla extract
- 1/2 cup sour cream
- 1/3 cup raspberry jam

Instructions:
1. Preheat the oven to 350°F (177°C).
2. In a medium bowl, mix together the graham cracker crumbs, melted butter, and 2 tablespoons of sugar.
3. Press the mixture into the bottom and up the sides of a 9-inch pie pan.
4. Bake for 10 minutes. Set aside to cool.
5. In a large bowl, beat the cream cheese until light and fluffy.
6. Gradually beat in the 1 cup of sugar.
7. Add the eggs, one at a time, mixing until incorporated.
8. Beat in the vanilla extract and sour cream.
9. Pour half of the batter into the cooled crust.
10. Spoon the raspberry jam over the batter.
11. Pour the remaining batter over the jam.
12. Swirl the jam using a knife.
13. Bake for 35-40 minutes or until the top is golden brown.
14. Cool for one hour before serving.

Nutrition information:
Calories: 271 kcal, Carbohydrates: 28 g, Protein: 3 g, Fat: 16 g, Saturated Fat: 9 g, Cholesterol: 74 mg, Sodium: 217 mg, Potassium: 73 mg, Fiber: 1 g, Sugar: 19 g, Vitamin A: 571 IU, Vitamin C: 1 mg, Calcium: 64 mg, Iron: 1 mg

71. Vegetable Pakoras

Vegetable Pakoras are a delicious Indian snack made from vegetables and a chickpea flour batter. They are deep-fried in oil to achieve the perfect crunchy texture.

Serving: 4

Preparation Time: 15 minutes

Ready Time: 40 minutes

Ingredients:
• 2 Cups gram flour
• 2 cups vegetables such as potatoes, cauliflower, or carrots, finely chopped
• 1 teaspoon red chili powder
• 1 teaspoon cumin powder
• Salt to taste
• Water
• Oil to deep fry

Instructions:
1. In a large bowl, mix together the gram flour, red chili powder, cumin powder, and salt.
2. Gradually add water to the flour mixture, stirring until a smooth, thick batter is formed.
3. Add the chopped vegetables and mix well until all the vegetables are well coated.
4. Heat oil in a deep pan over medium-high heat.
5. Scoop spoonfuls of the vegetable mixture into the hot oil and deep-fry until golden brown.
6. Remove the pakoras from the oil and drain on paper towels.
7. Serve warm with your favorite chutney or sauce.

Nutrition information: Calories – 180, Total Fat – 12 g, Cholesterol – 0 mg, Sodium – 300 mg, Total Carbohydrates – 12 g, Protein – 5 g.

72. Sticky Toffee Apple Cake

This Sticky Toffee Apple Cake is a tantalizing treat, made with moist caramel toffee cake infused with apples and sprinkled with pecans! Serves 8-10.

Serving: Serves 8-10

Preparation time: 20 minutes

Ready time: 50 minutes

Ingredients:
- ½ cup (1 stick) butter, softened
- 1 cup sugar
- 2 eggs
- 1 teaspoon pure vanilla extract
- 2 cups all-purpose flour
- 1 teaspoon baking powder
- ¼ teaspoon baking soda
- ¼ teaspoon salt
- 2 Granny Smith apples, peeled, cored and finely diced
- ½ cup diced pecans
- ½ cup toffee bits
- Caramel sauce for finishing

Instructions:
1. Preheat the oven to 350°F. Grease and flour a 9-by-13-inch cake pan and set aside.
2. In a medium bowl, cream together butter and sugar until fluffy. Add eggs and vanilla; beat until smooth.
3. In a separate bowl, sift together the flour, baking powder, baking soda, and salt. Slowly add the dry Ingredients to the wet Ingredients. Stir just until blended.
4. Fold in the apples, pecans, and toffee bits.
5. Transfer the batter to the prepared pan. Bake for 40 to 45 minutes, or until a toothpick inserted in the center comes out clean.
6. Let cool completely before topping with caramel sauce. Cut and serve.

Nutrition information:
Each slice of Sticky Toffee Apple Cake contains approximately 250 calories, 11 g fat, 34 g carbohydrates, and 3 g protein.

73. Lamb Seekh Kebabs

Lamb Seekh Kebabs are a delicious blend of ground lamb, spices, and herbs, creating a flavorful and juicy kebab.

Serving: 4-6
Preparation Time: 15 minutes
Ready Time: 30 minutes

Ingredients:
- 500g ground lamb
- 2 cloves of garlic, minced
- 1 teaspoon garam masala
- 1 teaspoon chili powder
- 1 teaspoon cumin powder
- 1 teaspoon paprika
- 1 teaspoon garam masala
- 1/2 cup freshly chopped cilantro
- 1 tablespoon olive oil
- Salt and pepper to taste

Instructions:
1. Place the ground lamb in a large bowl, and add the minced garlic, garam masala, chili powder, cumin powder, paprika, garam masala, cilantro, olive oil, salt, and pepper.
2. Mix all the Ingredients together until well combined.
3. Form the mixture into 8-10 patties.
4. Heat a grill or grill pan to medium-high heat.
5. Grill the kebabs for 4-5 minutes per side, flipping once, until cooked through.
6. Serve the kebabs with some fresh vegetables, a salad, and/or some warm naan.

Nutrition information:
Calories: 288 kcal,
Carbohydrates: 2 g,
Protein: 25 g,
Fat: 19 g,
Saturated Fat: 6 g,
Cholesterol: 72 mg,
Sodium: 103 mg,

Potassium: 327 mg,
Fiber: 1 g,
Sugar: 1 g,
Vitamin A: 521 IU,
Vitamin C: 1 mg,
Calcium: 42 mg,
Iron: 2 mg

74. Orange and Almond Cake

This Orange and Almond Cake is an aromatic treat that is sure to please the palate! Combining the tart citrusy flavor of oranges with the rich nutty taste of almonds, it is the perfect balance of sweet and sour.
Serving: 6-8
Preparation Time: 35 minutes
Ready Time: 1 hour 15 minutes

Ingredients:
- 3 oranges
- 2 cups sugar
- ½ cup vegetable oil
- 4 eggs
- 1 teaspoon vanilla
- 2 ½ cups all-purpose flour
- 1 teaspoon baking soda
- ½ teaspoon salt
- ½ cup almond meal
- Powdered sugar

Instructions:
1. Preheat oven to 350°F. Grease and flour a 9-inch round cake pan.
2. Zest 2 oranges, and squeeze the juice from the same oranges.
3. In a large bowl, cream together sugar and oil. Beat in eggs one at a time. Stir in vanilla, orange zest and juice and mix well.
4. In a separate bowl, sift together flour, baking soda, salt and almond meal.
5. Slowly add the flour mixture to the wet Ingredients, stirring until fully combined.

6. Pour the batter into the prepared pan and bake for 40-45 minutes, or until a toothpick inserted into the center comes out clean.

7. Let the cake cool for 15 minutes before transferring to a plate or platter.

8. Peel the third orange and slice it into thin rounds. Arrange the orange slices on top of the cake. Sprinkle with powdered sugar to finish.

Nutrition information: (per slice)
Calories: 337 kcal
Fat:14.2 g
Carbohydrates: 46.2 g
Protein: 4.3 g

75. Chicken Biryani Stuffed Zucchini

Try this delicious Chicken Biryani Stuffed Zucchini recipe for a unique take on the classic biryani dish. This flavorful dish combines zucchini, Indian-style spices, and shredded cooked chicken for a complete meal.
Serving: 4
Preparation time: 15 minutes
Ready Time: 45 minutes

Ingredients:
• 2 medium-sized zucchinis
• 2 tablespoons olive oil
• 1 pound cooked, shredded chicken
• 2 cups cooked basmati rice
• 1 medium onion, diced
• 2 cloves garlic, minced
• 1 teaspoon garam masala
• ½ teaspoon ground turmeric
• ¼ teaspoon ground cumin
• ½ teaspoon chili powder
• ¼ teaspoon ground cinnamon
• Salt and pepper to taste
• 2 tablespoons chopped fresh cilantro

Instructions:

1. Preheat oven to 375 degrees F (190 degrees C).
2. Cut the zucchinis in half lengthwise and scoop out the insides to form a boat. Place the hollowed-out zucchini halves in a baking dish.
3. Heat olive oil in a large skillet over medium-high heat. Add onion and garlic and cook, stirring occasionally, until softened, about 5 minutes.
4. Add shredded chicken, stirring to combine. Season with garam masala, turmeric, cumin, chili powder, cinnamon, and salt and pepper.
5. Place the cooked chicken mixture in the zucchini boats. Top each with cooked rice and sprinkle with cilantro.
6. Bake in preheated oven until the zucchini is tender and the tops are golden brown, about 30 minutes.

Nutrition information:
Calories: 409 kcal, Carbohydrates: 30 g, Protein: 35 g, Fat: 13 g, Saturated Fat: 2 g, Trans Fat: 1 g, Cholesterol: 87 mg, Sodium: 193 mg, Potassium: 688 mg, Fiber: 3 g, Sugar: 5 g, Vitamin A: 379 IU, Vitamin C: 24 mg, Calcium: 63 mg, Iron: 2 mg.

76. Chocolate Mousse

Chocolate Mousse is a delicious and easy-to-make dessert that you can make in the comfort of your own home. It's light and airy chocolate goodness that is sure to be a hit with everyone who tries it!
Serving: 6
Preparation Time: 10 minutes
Ready Time: 2 hours

Ingredients:
- 4 ounces semisweet chocolate, finely chopped
- 3 large eggs, separated
- 2 tablespoons white sugar
- 1/2 cup cold heavy cream
- 2 tablespoons unsalted butter

Instructions:
1. In a microwave-safe bowl, heat the chocolate and butter in 20 second intervals until melted and smooth. Allow to cool slightly.

2. In a medium bowl, beat the egg whites until frothy. Gradually add in the sugar, 1 tablespoon at a time, beating until the mixture is thick and glossy.

3. In a separate bowl, beat the egg yolks until pale and thick.

4. Gently fold the egg yolks into the melted chocolate.

5. In a separate bowl, whip the cream until stiff peaks form. Gently fold the cream into the chocolate mixture.

6. Finally, fold in the egg whites into the chocolate mixture until just combined.

7. Pour the mousse into individual serving dishes or into one large bowl. Refrigerate for at least 2 hours before serving.

Nutrition information: Calories: 225; Fat: 16g; Carbohydrate: 19g; Protein: 5g; Cholesterol: 90mg; Sodium:50 mg; Sugars: 17g.

77. Paneer Butter Masala

Paneer Butter Masala, a rich, creamy North Indian dish, is one of the most popular and beloved curries out there. It's made with marinated paneer (Indian cottage cheese), simmered in a creamy tomato and butter sauce.

Serving: 4
Preparation Time: 10 minutes
Ready Time: 25 minutes

Ingredients:
• 2 tablespoons of butter
• 1 teaspoon of cumin seeds
• 1 teaspoon of garam masala
• 2 cloves of garlic, minced
• 1 onion, chopped
• 1 tablespoon of grated ginger
• 2 teaspoons of paprika
• 1 teaspoon of turmeric
• 1 (14-ounce) can of diced tomatoes
• 2 tablespoons of tomato paste
• 1 (14-ounce) can of coconut milk
• 1/2 cup of heavy cream

• 2 tablespoons of honey
• 2 cups of paneer, cut into cubes
• 2 tablespoons of freshly chopped cilantro, for garnish

Instructions:
1. Heat the butter in a large skillet over medium-high heat.
2. Add the cumin seeds, garam masala, garlic, onion, ginger, paprika, and turmeric and cook, stirring, until the vegetables are soft and fragrant, about 5 minutes.
3. Add the diced tomatoes and tomato paste and stir to combine.
4. Add the coconut milk, heavy cream, and honey and bring to a simmer.
5. Add the paneer to the skillet and cook for 5 minutes.
6. Reduce the heat to low and simmer for 10 minutes.
7. Garnish with cilantro and serve.

Nutrition information:
Calories: 368, Total Fat: 24.1g, Saturated Fat: 15g, Carbohydrates: 15.6g, Protein: 19.3g, Sodium: 605mg, Potassium: 477mg, Fiber: 2.8g.

78. Mango and Coconut Lassi

Mango and Coconut Lassi is a refreshing drink, perfect to enjoy on a hot day. It is made from yogurt and coconut milk, combined with freshly pureed mango. It's a delicious and nutritious drink that is sure to satisfy your taste buds.
Serving: 4
Preparation time: 5 minutes
Ready time: 10 minutes

Ingredients:
- 2 cups plain yogurt
- 1 cup coconut milk
- 1 cup frozen mango chunks, thawed and drained
- 2 tablespoons honey
- 1/4 teaspoon ground cardamom

Instructions:

1. In a blender, combine yogurt, coconut milk, mango, honey and cardamom. Blend until smooth.
2. Pour the lassi into four glasses and serve.

Nutrition information:
Per Serving: Calories: 202, Fat: 7g, Carbohydrates: 25g, Protein: 7g, Sodium: 67mg

79. Chicken and Mushroom Pie

Chicken and Mushroom Pie is an unbeatable classic dinner dish that's sure to satisfy even the pickiest eaters. It's packed with chunks of juicy chicken and meaty mushrooms that are enveloped in a delicious, creamy white sauce. The combination of flavors and textures in this dish is simply unbeatable!
Serving: 4
Preparation time: 15 min
Ready time: 1 hr

Ingredients:
-4 tablespoons olive oil
-1 onion, finely chopped
-2 cloves garlic, minced
-1 lb chicken breasts, cut into cubes
-10 oz button mushrooms, sliced
-2 tablespoons all-purpose flour
-1 1/2 cups chicken stock
-1/4 cup dry white wine
-1 teaspoon dried thyme
-salt and black pepper to taste
-1 sheet frozen puff pastry, thawed
-1 egg, beaten

Instructions:
1. Preheat oven to 425°F (220°C).
2. Heat the oil in a large skillet over medium heat. Add the onion and garlic and cook, stirring occasionally, until the onion is softened, about 5 minutes.

3. Add the chicken and mushrooms and cook until the chicken is no longer pink, about 5 minutes.

4. Sprinkle the flour over the chicken and stir to coat. Slowly add the stock, wine, and thyme and season with salt and pepper to taste.

5. Pour the chicken and mushroom mixture into an 8" pie dish and cover with the puff pastry. Crimp the edges to seal.

6. Brush the pastry with the beaten egg and cut a few vents in the top.

7. Bake in preheated oven for 30-35 minutes until crust is golden brown and filling is bubbly.

Nutrition information: Per serving: Calories 480; Total Fat 22g; Sodium 834mg; Total Carbohydrates 30g; Sugars 4g; Protein 30g; Dietary Fiber 3g.

80. Lemon Poppy Seed Muffins

Lemon Poppy Seed Muffins are flavorful and moist muffins, infused with a hint of citrus and nutty poppy seeds.

Serving: 18 regular-sized muffins
Preparation Time: 15 minutes
Ready Time: 40 minutes

Ingredients:
-2 cups all-purpose flour
-1/4 cup poppyseeds
-2 teaspoons baking powder
-1/2 teaspoon salt
-2/3 cup granulated sugar
-1/3 cup canola oil
-1 large egg
-1/3 cup freshly squeezed lemon juice
-Zest of 1 lemon
-1/3 cup buttermilk

Instructions:
1. Preheat oven to 400°F (200°C).
2. Line muffin tin with paper liners or lightly grease.
3. In a bowl whisk together flour, poppy seeds, baking powder, and salt.

4. In another bowl whisk together sugar, oil, egg, lemon juice, zest and buttermilk.
5. Pour wet Ingredients into dry and mix until just combined.
6. Divide batter among muffin liners.
7. Bake for 18-20 minutes or until golden brown and toothpick inserted in center comes out clean.
8. Transfer to wire rack and let cool for 10 minutes.

Nutrition information:
Calories: 128 kcal, Carbohydrates:20 g, Protein: 2 g, Fat: 5 g, Sodium: 111 mg, Potassium: 62 mg, Fiber: 1 g, Sugar: 9 g, Vitamin A: 26 IU, Vitamin C: 2 mg, Calcium: 47 mg, Iron: 1 mg.

81. Vegetable Korma

Vegetable Korma is a rich and creamy curry dish made with mixed vegetables in a mildly spiced tomato and yogurt sauce. It is an incredibly popular dish from India and is a great vegetarian meal option.
Serving: 4 - 6 servings
Preparation time: 10 minutes
Ready time: 35 minutes

Ingredients:
• 2 tablespoons vegetable oil
• 1 onion, finely chopped
• 2 cloves garlic, minced
• 2 teaspoons ground coriander
• 1 teaspoon garam masala
• 1 teaspoon ground cumin
• 1/2 teaspoon ground turmeric
• 1 teaspoon ground ginger
• 1/2 teaspoon chilli powder
• 2 bay leaves
• 400g can diced tomatoes
• 1/2 cup vegetable stock
• 1 large sweet potato, peeled and diced
• 1 red capsicum, diced
• 1 cup cauliflower florets

- 2 carrots, peeled and diced
- 1/2 cup frozen peas
- 1/4 cup plain Greek yogurt
- Salt, to taste

Instructions:

1. Heat oil in a large saucepan over medium heat. Add the onion and garlic and cook until softened, about 5 minutes.
2. Add the spices and bay leaves to the onion mixture and cook for 1-2 minutes until fragrant.
3. Add the diced tomatoes, vegetable stock, sweet potato, capsicum, cauliflower and carrots to the pan and mix everything together.
4. Bring the mixture to a boil, then reduce the heat and simmer for 15 minutes, stirring occasionally.
5. Add the frozen peas and cook for an additional 5 minutes.
6. Remove the poriyal from the heat and stir in the Greek yogurt. Taste and add salt, if needed.
7. Serve over cooked basmati rice or chapati bread.

Nutrition information:

Calories:262 kcal, Carbohydrates:22.3g, Protein:5.8g, Fat:17.3g, Saturated Fat:9.2g, Cholesterol: 22mg, Sodium:35mg, Fiber:4.6g, Sugar:9.2g

82. Banoffee Pie

Banoffee Pie is a delicious, creamy, and rich dessert which combines sweet bananas, creamy toffee, and a crunchy biscuit crumb crust. This no-bake dessert is sure to become a family favorite.

Serving: 8-10

Preparation time: 5 minutes

Ready time: 2 hours

Ingredients:

- 1 packet digestive biscuits, crushed
- 3 tbsp melted butter
- 1 can condensed milk
- 375g dulche de leche
- 3 large bananas, peeled and sliced

- 2 cups whipping cream
- 2 tbsp icing sugar, sifted
- 1 tsp vanilla extract

Instructions:
1. Preheat the oven to 180°C (160°C fan-forced).
2. In a food processor or blender, blitz the digestive biscuits until they have a fine texture.
3. Add the melted butter and blitz until combined.
4. Grease a deep 23cm round baking tin and evenly press the biscuit mixture into the base and sides of it.
5. Bake for 10 minutes, then cool.
6. In a medium saucepan, heat the condensed milk and dulce de leche until combined, stirring often.
7. Spread the banana slices over the base of the cooled biscuit crust and pour the condensed milk and dulce de leche mixture over the top.
8. Refrigerate for 2 hours or until the mixture has set.
9. In a bowl, using an electric mixer or a whisk, whisk together the cream, icing sugar and vanilla extract until thick peaks form.
10. Spread the cream mixture over the pie and serve.

Nutrition information:
Calories: 465 kcal, Carbohydrates: 61 g, Protein: 5 g, Fat: 22 g, Saturated Fat: 11 g, Cholesterol: 62 mg, Sodium: 198 mg, Potassium: 291 mg, Fiber: 1 g, Sugar: 43 g, Vitamin A: 815 IU, Vitamin C: 4 mg, Calcium: 169 mg, Iron: 1 mg

83. Chicken Biryani Stuffed Tomatoes

Chicken Biryani Stuffed Tomatoes is a healthy and tasty chicken dish, cooked with basmati rice and stuffed into juicy tomatoes. This dish is full of flavor and will make a delicious addition to your meal.
Serving: 4
Preparation Time: 10 minutes
Ready Time: 25 minutes

Ingredients:
• 4 medium-sized tomatoes

- 1/2 cup cooked chicken biryani
- 1/4 cup crumbled feta cheese
- 2 tablespoons minced green onion
- 2 tablespoons olive oil
- 1/2 teaspoon ground cumin
- 1/4 teaspoon each of coriander, chili powder and turmeric powder
- Salt to taste
- 2 tablespoons chopped cilantro

Instructions:
1. Preheat oven to 375 degrees F.
2. Cut the tops off the tomatoes and scoop out the pulp, leaving the shells intact. Set shells aside.
3. In a bowl, mix together the chicken biryani, feta cheese, green onion, olive oil, cumin, coriander, chili powder, turmeric powder, salt and cilantro.
4. Fill each tomato shell with the biryani mixture and top with a sprinkle of cilantro.
5. Place tomatoes on a baking sheet and bake for 15 minutes.
6. Serve hot.

Nutrition information:
Per Serving: 190 calories, 12 g of fat, 9 g of carbohydrate, 10 g of protein

84. Chocolate Hazelnut Tart

This decadent Chocolate Hazelnut Tart is a delicious combination of rich chocolate and crunchy hazelnuts, all held together by a tender shortbread crust.
Serving: 8-10 portions
Preparation time: 15 minutes
Ready time: 1 hour

Ingredients:
- 200g hazelnuts
- 110g unsalted butter
- 70g sugar
- 28g cocoa powder

- 28g all-purpose flour
- 2 tsp vanilla extract
- 150g dark chocolate

Instructions:
1. Preheat the oven to 180C/ 350F degrees.
2. Roast the hazelnuts in the oven or in a pan over medium heat for 8 minutes, or until golden brown. Set aside to cool.
3. In a medium bowl, mix together the butter, sugar, cocoa powder, flour, and vanilla extract until the Ingredients are fully incorporated and the dough is thick and crumbly.
4. Grease a tart pan with butter or cooking spray and press the dough into the bottom and sides of the pan.
3. Place in the preheated oven and bake for 15 minutes.
4. Remove from the oven and cool for 15 minutes.
5. Break the dark chocolate into pieces and place in a medium heatproof bowl.
6. Add the roasted hazelnuts and mix until combined.
7. Spread the chocolate and hazelnut mixture into the tart and bake for an additional 40 minutes.
8. Remove from the oven and let cool completely before serving.

Nutrition information: Per Serving – Calories: 325, Fat: 21g, Carbs: 27g, Protein: 6g

85. Lamb Bhuna

Lamb Bhuna is a traditional Indian dish. It is a delicious, spicy, and flavorful meal that is popular in Indian households. It is best enjoyed with steamed basmati rice or roti (Indian flatbread).
Serving: 4
Preparation time: 10 minutes
Ready time: 40 minutes

Ingredients:
- 1 kilogram of lamb shoulder, cubed
- 2-3 tablespoons of vegetable or sunflower oil
- 2 onion, finely chopped

- 2 large cloves of garlic, grated or minced
- 1 tablespoon of grated ginger
- 1 teaspoon of cumin seeds
- 2 teaspoons of ground coriander
- 1 teaspoon of garam masala
- 1 teaspoon of chilli powder
- 2 large tomatoes, chopped
- 2 tablespoons of tomato puree
- ½ teaspoon of sugar
- Salt to taste

Instructions:
1. Heat the oil in a large saucepan over a medium-high heat.
2. Add the onion, garlic, and ginger. Cook, stirring often, until the onion is beginning to soften.
3. Add the cumin seeds, stirring for a few minutes until they become fragrant.
4. Add the ground coriander, garam masala, and chilli powder. Cook for a further minute.
5. Add the cubed lamb. Cook, stirring, until the lamb turns golden brown.
6. Add the chopped tomatoes, tomato puree, sugar, and salt. Stir to combine.
7. Reduce the heat to low and cook, stirring occasionally, for around 30 minutes or until the lamb is tender and cooked through.

Nutrition information: Per serving: Calories 384, Fat 17g, Saturated Fat upon 5g, Protein 38g, Carbohydrates 12g, Fiber 4g, Sugar 5g, Salt 1.6g.

86. Raspberry and Coconut Scones

These Raspberry and Coconut Scones are light and fluffy, and full of flavor. The combination of raspberries and coconut adds a yummy texture and natural sweetness to these scones. Enjoy them warm from the oven with a fresh cup of coffee.
Serving: 8-10
Preparation time: 20 minutes

Ready time: 35 minutes

Ingredients:
- 2 cups all-purpose flour
- ⅓ cup sugar
- 1 tablespoon baking powder
- ½ teaspoon salt
- 5 tablespoons cold butter, cubed
- ¾ cup shredded coconut
- ⅓ cup half-and-half or cold milk
- 1 cup fresh raspberries

Instructions:
1. Preheat the oven to 425°F. Line a baking sheet with parchment paper.
2. In a large bowl, whisk together flour, sugar, baking powder and salt until combined.
3. Using a pastry blender or a fork, cut in butter until it resembles coarse meal.
4. Stir in coconut, half-and-half (or milk) and the raspberries until just combined.
5. Turn the dough out onto a lightly floured work surface and knead once or twice.
6. Pat into a 7-inch circle. Cut into 8 wedges and transfer onto the baking sheet.
7. Bake in preheated oven for 12-15 minutes, or until the top is golden brown.

Nutrition information:
Calories: 199
Fat: 10.8 g
Carbohydrates: 24.5 g
Protein: 3.2 g

87. Chicken Curry Puffs

Chicken Curry Puffs are an Indian dish commonly served as an appetizer. These flavor-packed snacks are made with chunky curry chicken generously coated in a light and flaky crust. Delicious and incredibly easy to make, these chicken curry puffs make for a great appetizer or a quick snack.

Serving: Makes 12-15 curry puffs
Preparation time: 10 -15 minutes
Ready time: 25 minutes

Ingredients:
-1 cup cooked and shredded chicken
-1 teaspoon minced garlic
-1 teaspoon grated ginger
-1 teaspoon chili powder
-1 teaspoon garam masala
-1 teaspoon ground coriander
-1 teaspoon ground cumin
-1/4 teaspoon ground turmeric
-1/4 teaspoon ground nutmeg
-1/2 teaspoon ground cardamom
-2 green chilies, minced
-2 tablespoons olive oil
-1/4 cup finely chopped onion
-2 tablespoons chopped fresh coriander leaves
-2 tablespoons raisins
-2 tablespoons slivered almonds
-1/4 cup coconut flakes
-1/2 package puff pastry dough, thawed
-1 egg, beaten

Instructions:
1. In a large bowl, combine chicken, garlic, ginger, chili powder, garam masala, coriander, cumin, turmeric, nutmeg, and cardamom.
2. Heat the olive oil in a large skillet over medium heat. Add the onion and cook for 3-4 minutes, until softened.
3. Add the chicken mixture to the skillet and stir to combine. Cook for 5-7 minutes, until the chicken is cooked through and the spices are fragrant.
4. Remove the skillet from the heat and add the fresh coriander leaves, raisins, almonds, and coconut flakes. Stir to combine.
5. Preheat the oven to 375 degrees F. Line a large baking sheet with parchment paper and set aside.

6. On a lightly floured surface, roll out the puff pastry dough into a 12 x 15-inch rectangle. Cut out circles with a 3-inch biscuit cutter.
7. Place 1 tablespoon of the chicken mixture onto the center of each dough circle.
8. Brush the edges of the dough with the beaten egg, then fold them over and press to seal. Place the curry puffs onto the prepared baking sheet.
9. Brush the curry puffs with the remaining beaten egg.
10. Bake for 15-20 minutes, until golden brown.

Nutrition information: Per Serving (1 curry puff): 135 Calories, 6.7 g Fat, 12.8 g Carbohydrates, 2.1 g Fiber, 4.3 g Protein

88. Blueberry Crumble Bars

These Blueberry Crumble Bars are a sweet and tart snack that is perfect to take to potlucks and holiday parties. It is a delicious combination of sweet and salty flavors!
Serving: 12
Preparation time: 15 minutes
Ready time: 1 hour

Ingredients:
- 2 cups all-purpose flour
- 1/2 cup packed light brown sugar
- 1 teaspoon baking powder
- 1/2 teaspoon baking soda
- 1/2 teaspoon salt
- 1/2 cup (1 stick) cold butter, cubed
- 2 large eggs
- 2 teaspoon pure vanilla extract
- 2 cups fresh blueberries
- 1/4 cup sugar

Instructions:
1. Preheat the oven to 350°F. Grease a 9x13 inch baking pan.
2. In a medium bowl, whisk together the flour, brown sugar, baking powder, baking soda, and salt.

3. Cut in the butter with a pastry blender or two knives until it resembles coarse crumbs.

4. Place the mixture in the prepared pan and gently press it into an even layer.

5. In a separate bowl, whisk the eggs and vanilla. Pour the egg mixture over the dry Ingredients and spread evenly.

6. Top with blueberries and sprinkle with sugar.

7. Bake for about 40 minutes, or until golden brown. Allow to cool completely before cutting into bars.

Nutrition information:
Calories – 163 kcal - per Serving: Total fat – 7 g - per Serving: Carbohydrate – 22 g - per Serving: Protein – 2 g - per serving

89. Fish Curry

Fish curry is a classic Indian dish that is full of flavor and is easy to make. It is a simple dish that requires few Ingredients. This dish is great when served with steamed rice or naan bread.

Serving: 6
Preparation Time: 10 minutes
Ready Time: 30 minutes

Ingredients:
• 2 tablespoons of oil
• 2 small onions (diced)
• 1 teaspoon of ginger (grated)
• 1 teaspoon of garlic (grated)
• 2 teaspoons of ground coriander
• 1 teaspoon of ground cumin
• 2 tablespoons of tomato paste
• 1/2 teaspoon of chili powder (or more to taste)
• 1 teaspoon of turmeric
• 2 tablespoons of lemon juice
• 1 lbs of fish fillets (cut into cubes)
• 1 cup of coconut milk
• 1 teaspoon of sugar
• Salt to taste

Instructions:

1. In a large pot, heat oil over medium heat. Add in diced onions and cook for 2-3 minutes until softened.
2. Add in grated ginger and garlic and stir for a minute or two.
3. Add in coriander, cumin, tomato paste, chili powder, turmeric, and lemon juice. Stir until spices are well combined.
4. Add in the fish cubes and season with salt.
5. Pour in the coconut milk and add the sugar.
6. Reduce heat and simmer for 15-20 minutes, stirring occasionally.
7. Taste and adjust the seasoning if needed.
8. Serve with steamed rice or naan bread and enjoy!

Nutrition information:

Calories: 224
Fat: 11.5g
Carbs: 4.3g
Protein: 18.1g

90. Strawberry Shortcake

This delicious Strawberry Shortcake recipe is a classic summer dessert. It's light, fluffy, and bursting with juicy strawberries – everyone is sure to love it!

Serving: 4-6 servings
Preparation Time: 10 minutes
Ready Time: 20 minutes

Ingredients:

- 2 cups all-purpose flour
- 1/2 cup white sugar
- 2 1/2 teaspoons baking powder
- 1/2 teaspoon salt
- 1/2 cup cold butter, cubed
- 2/3 cup milk
- 3 cups fresh strawberries, sliced
- 1/3 cup white sugar
- 1 cup whipping cream

- 2 tablespoons white sugar

Instructions:
1. Preheat oven to 375 degrees F (190 degrees C). Grease an 8 inch cake pan.
2. In a medium bowl, mix together flour, 1/2 cup sugar, baking powder and salt. Cut in butter until mixture resembles coarse crumbs. Stir in milk. Spread evenly into the prepared pan.
3. Bake in preheated oven for 20 minutes, or until a toothpick inserted in the center of the cake comes out clean. Let cool in the pan, about 10 minutes.
4. In a medium bowl, mix together sliced strawberries and 1/3 cup sugar.
5. In a medium bowl, beat whipping cream until it begins to thicken. Gradually add 2 tablespoons sugar, and continue beating until stiff peaks form.
6. Place cake on a serving plate. Top with strawberries, followed by whipped cream.

Nutrition information: (per serving) 292 calories; 11.7 g fat; 40.3 g carbohydrates; 4 g protein; 109 mg sodium.

91. Vegetable Biryani Stuffed Peppers

Food lovers, this Vegetable Biryani Stuffed Peppers recipe is the perfect combination of Indian spices and fresh vegetables for a vibrant and flavorful meal.
Serving: Serves 3
Preparation Time: 15 minutes
Ready Time: 25 minutes

Ingredients:
- 1 tsp garlic paste
- 1 tsp ginger paste
- 1/2 cup vegetable stock
- 1 1/2 cups cooked rice
- 1/2 cup diced bell pepper
- 1/2 cup diced onion
- 1/2 cup diced carrots

- 1/2 cup diced green beans
- 1/2 cup cooked peas
- 2 tbsp chopped cilantro
- 1 tsp garam masala
- 1/4 tsp turmeric
- 1/2 tsp cumin powder
- 1/4 tsp coriander powder
- 3 bell peppers
- 2 tsp vegetable oil

Instructions:
1. Preheat oven to 375°F.
2. Heat oil in a large skillet over medium heat.
3. Add garlic and ginger paste, and cook for 2 minutes.
4. Add bell pepper, onion, carrots, green beans, and cook for 3-4 minutes.
5. Add cooked peas to the skillet.
6. Add the cooked rice, vegetable stock, garam masala, turmeric, cumin powder, and coriander powder, and stir to combine.
7. Remove from heat, add chopped cilantro, and mix well.
8. Cut the tops off the bell peppers and scoop out the insides.
9. Stuff the bell peppers with the cooked biryani mixture.
10. Place the stuffed bell peppers in a greased baking dish.
11. Bake in preheated oven for 20 minutes, or until the bell peppers are tender.

Nutrition information: (per serving)
Calories: 320 kcal
Carbohydrates: 54.6g
Protein: 6.8g
Fat: 9.4g
Saturated fat: 1.2g
Sodium: 277mg
Fiber: 7.2g

92. Lemon Blueberry Loaf

Lemon Blueberry Loaf is a delightful and refreshing sweet snack made with lemons and fresh blueberries. This is a delicious and easy to make loaf that is perfect for a summer picnic, barbeque, or even just a special treat.

Serving: 12

Preparation time: 10 Minutes

Ready time: 45 Minutes

Ingredients:
- 2 cups all-purpose flour
- 1 teaspoon baking powder
- 1/2 teaspoon baking soda
- 1/4 teaspoon salt
- 2/3 cup white sugar
- 1/2 cup vegetable oil
- 2 eggs
- 2 tablespoons lemon zest
- 1/4 cup freshly squeezed lemon juice
- 1 cup fresh blueberries

Instructions:
1. Preheat the oven to 350°F (175°C). Grease and lightly flour a 9x5 inch loaf pan.
2. In a medium bowl mix together the flour, baking powder, baking soda, and salt.
3. In a large bowl cream together the sugar and oil. Beat in the eggs, one at a time, then stir in the lemon zest and juice.
4. Gradually mix in the dry Ingredients until just blended. Gently fold in the blueberries.
5. Pour batter into the greased loaf pan and bake for 40-45 minutes in the preheated oven, or until a knife inserted into the center of the loaf comes out clean.

Nutrition information: Calories: 256, Total Fat: 11.7g, Saturated Fat: 1.8g, Polyunsaturated Fat: 9.5g, Monounsaturated Fat: .6g, Sodium: 103mg, Potassium: 65mg, Total Carbohydrates: 34.7g, Dietary Fiber: .8g, Sugars: 18.4g, Protein: 3.6g

93. Lamb Vindaloo

Lamb Vindaloo is a classic Indian dish made with marinated lamb cooked in a spiced tomato gravy. The dish has its origins in Goa and is popular in other parts of India as well.

Serving: 4-6
Preparation time: 15 minutes
Ready time: 1 hour

Ingredients:
-1 lb boneless lamb, cut into cubes
-3 medium tomatoes, chopped
-2 tablespoons oil
-1 medium onion, finely chopped
-1 green chilli, chopped
-2 tablespoons ginger-garlic paste
-1 teaspoon cumin powder
-1 teaspoon coriander powder
-2 tablespoons red chilli powder
-1 teaspoon garam masala
-1 teaspoon turmeric powder
-2 tablespoons vinegar
-Salt according to taste
-Fresh coriander leaves for garnish

Instructions:
1. In a large bowl mix together the lamb cubes, ginger-garlic paste, vinegar, 1 teaspoon of the red chilli powder, and salt to taste. Set aside for 15 minutes.
2. Heat the oil in a large pan over medium heat. Add the chopped onion and green chilli and cook until the onion is lightly browned.
3. Add the cumin, coriander, red chilli, garam masala, and turmeric powder to the pan and fry for a few seconds.
4. Add the tomato to the pan and cook for a few more minutes until the tomatoes are softened.
5. Add the marinated lamb to the pan and mix until combined. Cover the pan and cook for 20-30 minutes, stirring occasionally.
6. Once the lamb is cooked through, remove the lid and continue to simmer until the sauce has thickened.
7. Garnish with fresh coriander leaves.

Nutrition information:
Calories: 447 kcal, Carbohydrates: 17g, Protein: 23g, Fat: 30g, Saturated Fat: 9g, Cholesterol: 80mg, Sodium: 129mg, Potassium: 579mg, Fiber: 3g, Sugar: 6g, Vitamin A: 835IU, Vitamin C: 19.3mg, Calcium: 79mg, Iron: 4.3mg

94. Mango and Passion Fruit Fool

Mango and Passion Fruit Fool is a light and delicious summer dessert. It's easy to make and packed with flavor.
Serving: 4
Preparation time: 10 minutes
Ready time: 40 minutes

Ingredients:
- 2 ripe mangos, peeled and diced
- 2 passion fruits, pulp and seeds
- 1 tablespoon honey
- ½ cup Greek yogurt
- 2 tablespoons fresh mint, chopped

Instructions:
1. In a medium bowl, combine the mangos, passion fruit pulp and seeds, honey and yogurt.
2. Stir gently until all Ingredients are combined.
3. Place the mixture into four individual serving dishes or one large bowl.
4. Sprinkle the mint over the top and chill in the refrigerator for at least 30 minutes.
5. Serve chilled.

Nutrition information:
Calories: 150, Protein: 6 g, Total fat: 2 g, Sodium: 15 mg, Total carbs: 28 g, Fiber: 4 g, Sugar: 18 g

95. Chicken Biryani Stuffed Eggplant

Chicken Biryani Stuffed Eggplant is a delicious and flavorful entrée perfect for any occasion. This dish is made by stuffing eggplants with a rich and savory chicken biryani filing before roasting them in the oven.
Serving: 4
Preparation Time: 10 minutes
Ready Time: 45 minutes

Ingredients:
• 2 large eggplants
• 2 cups cooked chicken biryani
• 2 tablespoons olive oil
• 1 teaspoon minced garlic
• Salt and pepper, to taste
• 2 tablespoons chopped fresh cilantro

Instructions:
1. Preheat the oven to 375 degrees F.
2. Cut the eggplants in half lengthwise and scoop out the insides, creating a boat shape.
3. Place the eggplant halves on a baking sheet and brush with the olive oil.
4. Sprinkle with the garlic, salt, and pepper.
5. Stuff the eggplants with the chicken biryani.
6. Bake in the preheated oven for 30-35 minutes, or until the eggplant is cooked through and golden brown.
7. Garnish with fresh cilantro and serve.

Nutrition information: Calories 341, Total Fat 16g, Saturated Fat 3g, Cholesterol 89mg, Sodium 397mg, Total Carbohydrates 16g, Dietary Fiber 5g, Protein 33g.

96. Chocolate Caramel Slice

Chocolate Caramel Slice is a tasty and decadent treat combining the delicious flavor of chocolate and rich sweetness of caramel. Its creamy layers of chocolate, shortbread base, and sticky caramel topping make it irresistible.
Serving: 16 slices

Preparation time: 30 minutes
Ready time: 2 hours

Ingredients:
- 1 ½ cups plain flour
- ¾ cup desiccated coconut
- 115g butter, melted
- 2 tablespoons of golden syrup
- 395g can of condensed milk
- 3 tablespoons of cocoa
- 200g of dark cooking chocolate
- 50g butter
- 2 tablespoons of golden syrup
- 2 tablespoons of brown sugar

Instructions:
1. Preheat oven to 165°C.
2. Grease and line an 18x28cm lamington tin with baking paper.
3. For the base, combine the flour, coconut, melted butter and golden syrup together in a bowl. Press the mixture into the prepared tin and bake for 20 minutes.
4. To make the caramel, combine the condensed milk, cocoa, butter, golden syrup and brown sugar in a medium saucepan and stir over a low heat until thick and creamy.
5. Pour the caramel over the cooled base and spread it evenly. Allow the slice to cool before topping with the melted chocolate.
6. To melt the chocolate, add the chocolate to a double saucepan and once it has melted, spread it over the cooled slice.
7. Allow to cool completely before slicing.

Nutrition information: Per Serving (1 slice): 237 calories, 12.5g of fat, 28g of carbohydrates.

97. Paneer Tikka Masala

Paneer Tikka Masala is a popular Indian dish, featuring cubes of paneer marinated in spices and finished in a creamy tomato-based sauce. It is served with basmati rice or naan bread.

Serving: 4
Preparation Time: 30 minutes
Ready Time: 1 hour

Ingredients:
- 10-15 cubes of paneer
- 1 teaspoon cumin powder
- 2 teaspoons coriander powder
- 1 teaspoon garam masala
- 2 tablespoons olive oil
- 1 teaspoon red chilli powder
- 2 tomatoes, diced
- ½ cup cream or yogurt
- 2 tablespoons butter
- 1 large onion, sliced
- 2 cloves garlic, minced
- 1 tablespoon freshly chopped ginger
- 2 tablespoons freshly chopped coriander leaves
- Salt to taste

Instructions:
1. Begin by making the marinade. Place the cumin powder, coriander powder, garam masala, red chilli powder and a pinch of salt in a small bowl and mix.
2. Take the paneer cubes and rub the marinade into them; allow to sit for at least 10 minutes.
3. Heat the olive oil in a large skillet over medium-high heat. Once hot, add the marinated paneer cubes and cook until they are lightly golden brown.
4. Remove the paneer cubes from the skillet and set aside.
5. In the same skillet, melt the butter and add the onion slices, garlic and ginger. Cook until the onions are translucent.
6. Add the diced tomatoes and let simmer for 5 minutes or so.
7. Return the paneer cubes to the skillet and add the cream or yogurt.
8. Stir everything together and allow to simmer for 20 minutes.
9. Sprinkle with freshly chopped coriander leaves and serve with basmati rice or naan bread.

Nutrition information: Paneer Tikka Masala provides approximately 250 calories per serving, and contains protein,

carbohydrates, fiber, fat, and several essential vitamins and minerals.

98. Pistachio Baklava

Pistachio Baklava is a classic Mediterranean pastry made with layers of flaky phyllo dough, filled with a delicious nut mixture, sweetened and held together with butter and honey syrup.
Serving: Allows to serve 9 people
Preparation time: 25 minutes
Ready time: 75 minutes

Ingredients:
- 3/4 cup (90 g) unsalted shelled pistachios
- 1/4 cup (50 g) granulated sugar
- 1 teaspoon ground cardamom
- 16 sheets of phyllo pastry
- 10 tablespoons (140 g) melted butter
- 1/2 cup (120 ml) honey
- 2 tablespoons (30 ml) lemon juice
- 2 tablespoons (30 ml) water

Instructions:
1. Preheat the oven to 350°F (180°C).
2. In a food processor, combine the pistachios, sugar, and cardamom and pulse until the pistachios are finely ground.
3. Grease a 9-inch (22 cm) square baking pan and lay a sheet of parchment paper in the bottom.
4. Layer 8 sheets of phyllo pastry in the pan, brushing each sheet with melted butter.
5. Spread the pistachio mixture evenly over the top.
6. Layer the remaining 8 sheets of pastry on top, brushing each sheet with more melted butter.
7. Cut the baklava into 9 equal squares or diamonds.
8. Bake for 45 minutes, or until golden brown.
9. While the baklava is baking, make the honey syrup by combining the honey, lemon juice, and water in a small saucepan.

10. Simmer the mixture for 5 minutes, stirring frequently, then remove it from the heat.

11. Remove the baklava from the oven and pour the honey syrup overtop.

12. Let the baklava sit for 30 minutes before serving.

Nutrition information: per slices- Calories: 248 Kcal, Total fat: 14.9g, Saturated fat: 8.3g, Carbohydrates: 28.9g, Sugar: 16.2g, Protein: 3.2g, Sodium: 35mg.

CONCLUSION

Nadiya Hussain's debut cookbook, Nadiya's Kitchen, is an amazing collection of 98 tasty recipes, suitable for the whole family. Throughout the book, Hussain has managed to make cooking a family affair, involving everyone from children to grandparents in the process of preparing delicious meals.

In her simple and approachable style, Hussain presents meal ideas suitable for everyone from busy mums to students on a budget, as well as ideas for special occasions like Sunday lunches and party snacks. Each recipe is accompanied by detailed step-by-step instructions as well as helpful hints and tips to make sure that cooking is an enjoyable experience.

Most importantly, Hussain has managed to create a cookbook that appeals to everyone, regardless of their cooking skills. From beginner cooks to experienced chefs, Nadiya's Kitchen will be sure to inspire and motivate. With its mix of flavours and textures, every recipe offers something new and exciting.

Hussain has really put a personal touch to her cookbook with her stories and anecdotes, making it all the more inspiring and inviting. More than just a collection of recipes, it really feels like a conversation with a friend. Reading her book will make you feel like you're getting cozy in the kitchen with Nadiya herself.

Nadiya Hussain is truly a master of the kitchen and it is highly evident in her cookbook, Nadiya's Kitchen. Each recipe is carefully crafted to ensure that it is not only delicious, but also contains balanced nutrition. Hussain ensures that each meal is packed with flavor while still being relatively simple to make.

The book is a fun and informative collection of recipes suitable for everyone in the family. Hussain's vibrant and inviting tone makes it a pleasure to read, and it is hard to come away from the book without feeling inspired. Whether you are a novice cook or a seasoned chef, Nadiya's Kitchen will give you the tools to create something magical.

Printed in Great Britain
by Amazon